TATTOOS
TRADITIONAL

TATOUAGES
TRADITIONNELS

"NOT ONE GREAT COUNTRY CAN BE NAMED, FROM THE POLAR REGIONS IN THE NORTH TO NEW ZEALAND IN THE SOUTH, IN WHICH THE ABORIGINES DO NOT TATTOO THEMSELVES."

(CHARLES DARWIN, ON THE DESCENT OF MAN)

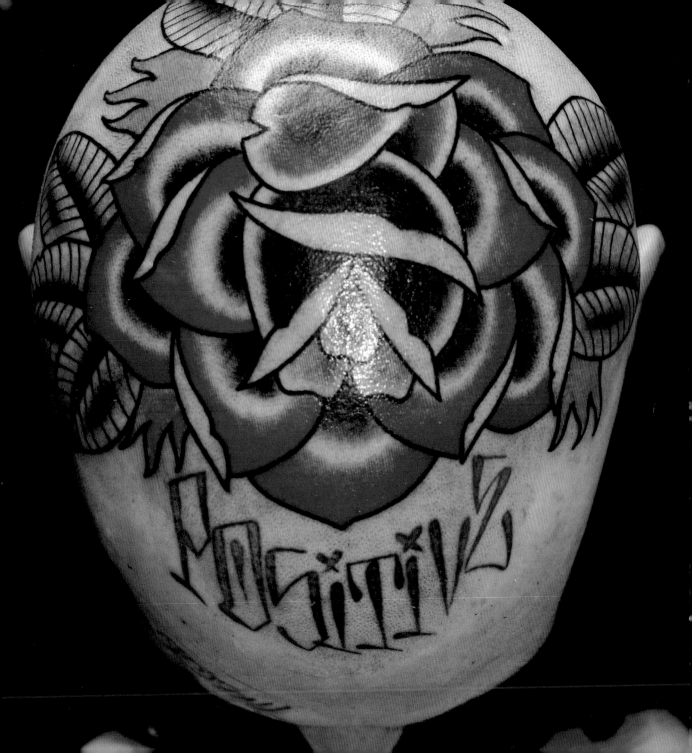

« ON NE PEUT CITER AUCUN GRAND PAYS, DES
RÉGIONS POLAIRES DU NORD JUSQU'EN
NOUVELLE ZÉLANDE AU SUD, DANS LEQUEL LES
AUTOCHTONES NE SERAIENT PAS TATOUÉS »

(CHARLES DARWIN, SUR L'ORIGINE DE L'HOMME)

"NICHT EIN EINZIGES GROSSES LAND VON DEN POLARGEGENDEN IM NORDEN BIS NACH NEUSEELAND IM SÜDEN KANN ANGEFÜHRT WERDEN, IN WELCHEM DIE URSPRÜNGLICHEN BEWOHNER SICH NICHT TÄTOWIERT HÄTTEN"

(CHARLES DARWIN, ÜBER DIE ABSTAMMUNG DES MENSCHEN)

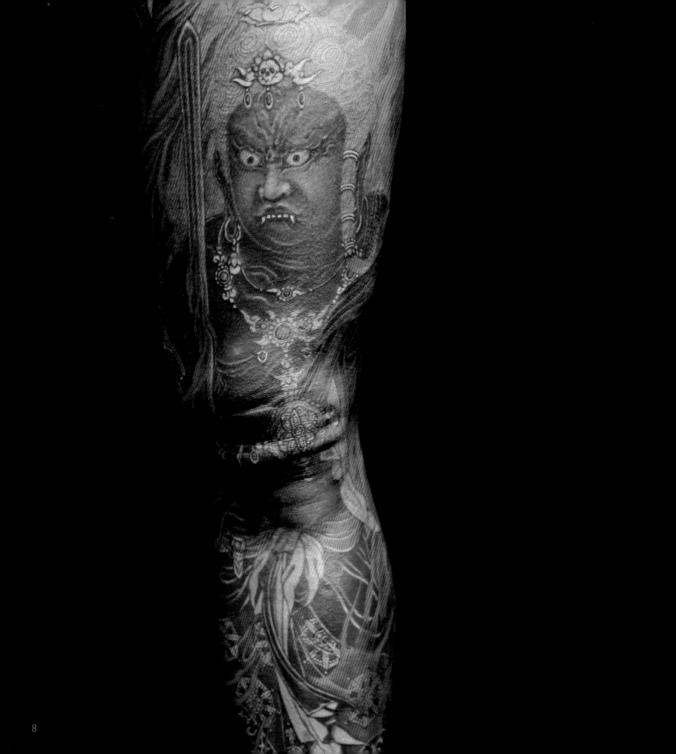

VAN DE POOLGEBIEDEN IN HET NOORDEN TOT
NIEUW-ZEELAND IN HET ZUIDEN KAN GEEN ENKEL LAND
WORDEN GENOEMD WAAR DE OORSPRONKELIJKE
BEWONERS GEEN TATOEAGES HEBBEN"

(CHARLES DARWIN, OVER DE AFSTAMMING VAN DE MENS)

«NO PUEDE NOMBRARSE NI UN SOLO GRAN PAÍS, DESDE LAS REGIONES POLARES EN EL NORTE HASTA NUEVA ZELANDA EN EL SUR, EN EL QUE SUS ABORÍGENES NO SE HAYAN TATUADO.»

(CHARLES DARWIN, SOBRE EL ORIGEN DEL HOMBRE)

"NON SI PUÒ MENZIONARE UN GRANDE PAESE, DALLE REGIONI POLARI A SETTENTRIONE FINO ALLA NUOVA ZELANDA A MEZZOGIORNO, IN CUI GLI INDIGENI NON SOGLIONO SCREZIARSI LA PELLE COL COSIDDETTO TATUAGGIO"

(CHARLES DARWIN, L'ORIGINE DELL'UOMO)

"NÃO É POSSÍVEL MENCIONAR UM ÚNICO PAÍS, DAS REGIÕES POLARES DO NORTE ATÉ A NOVA ZELÂNDIA, NO QUAL OS ABORÍGENAS NÃO SE TIVESSEM TATUADO"

(CHARLES DARWIN, A ORIGEM DO HOMEM)

"DET FINNS INGET STORT LAND FRÅN POLAROMRÅDENA
I NORR TILL NYA ZEELAND I SÖDER,
DÄR DEN URSPRUNGLIGA BEFOLKNINGEN
INTE HAR TATUERAT SIG"

(CHARLES DARWIN, MÄNNISKANS HÄRLEDNING)

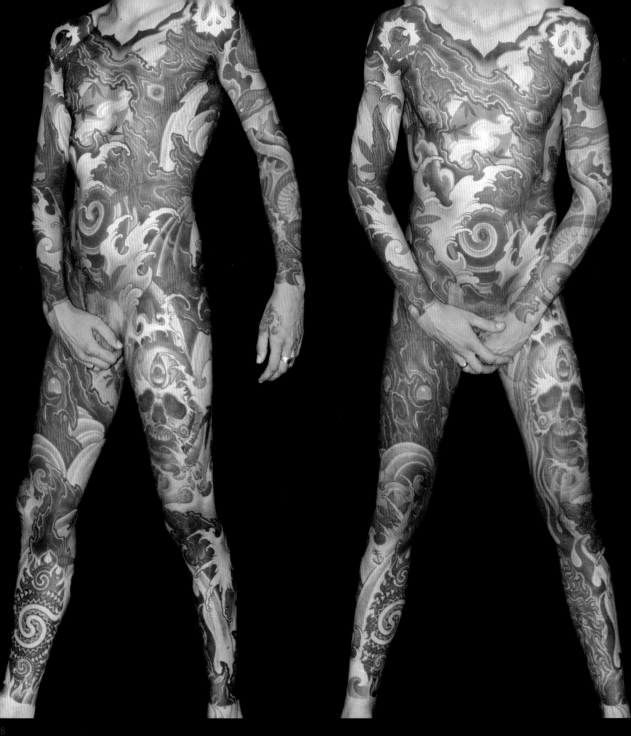

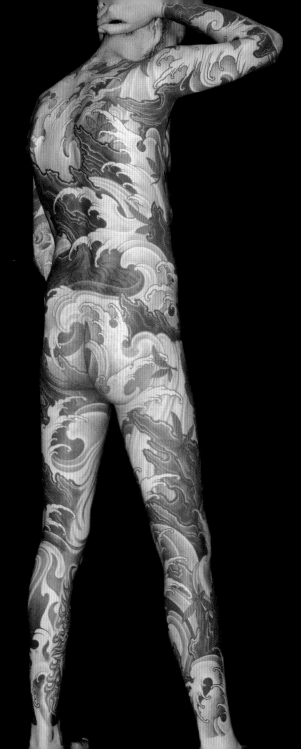

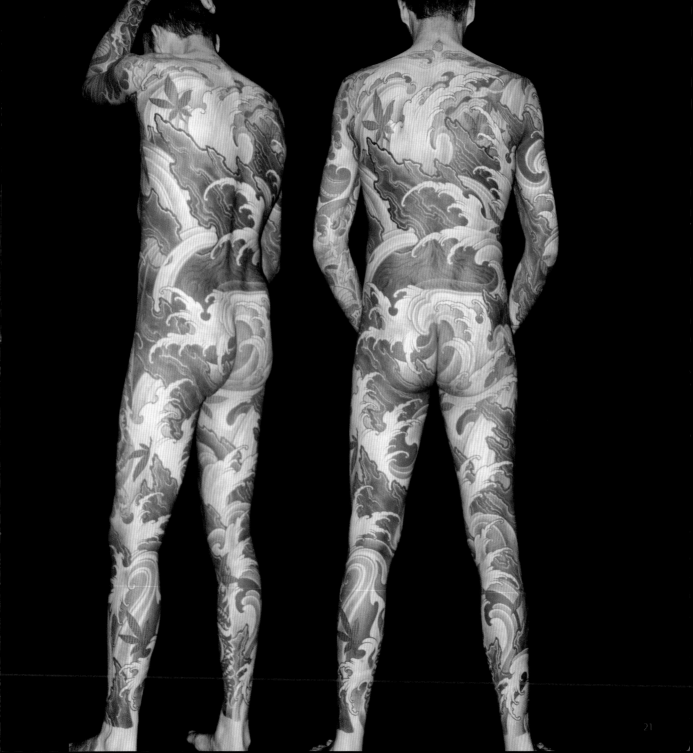

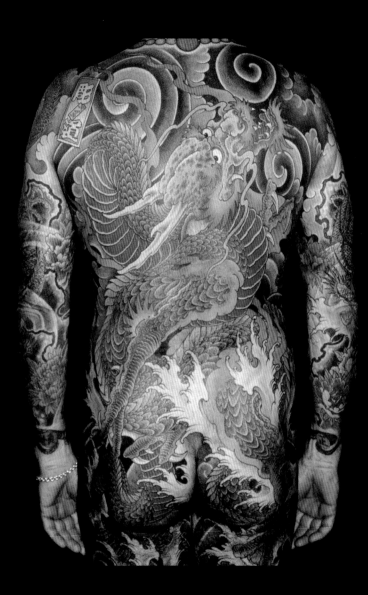

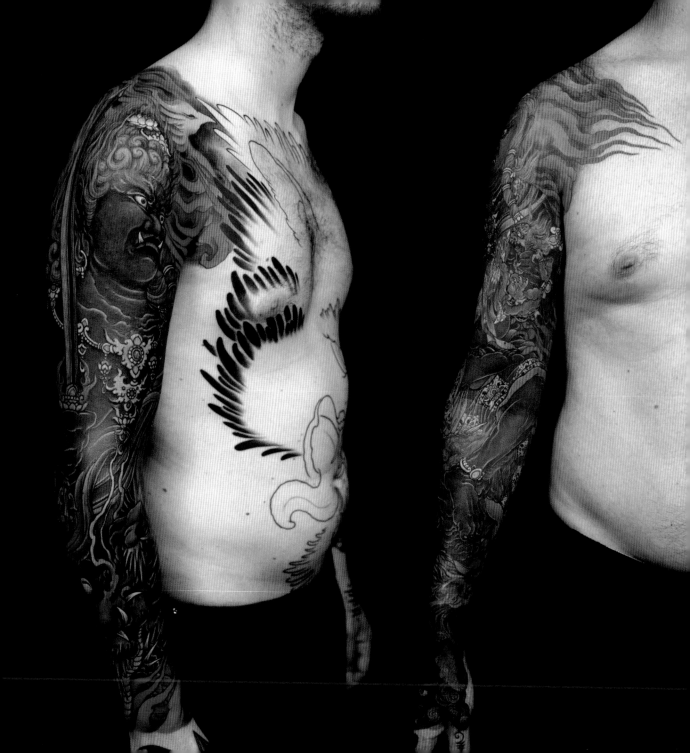

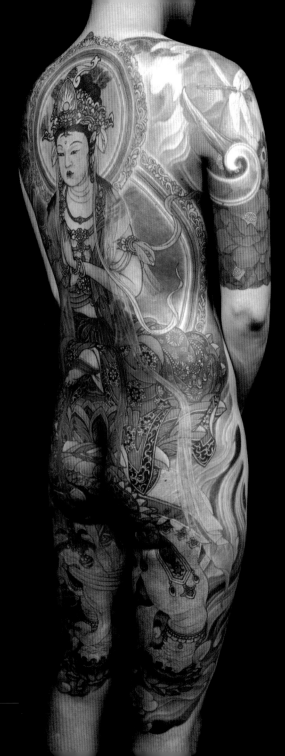

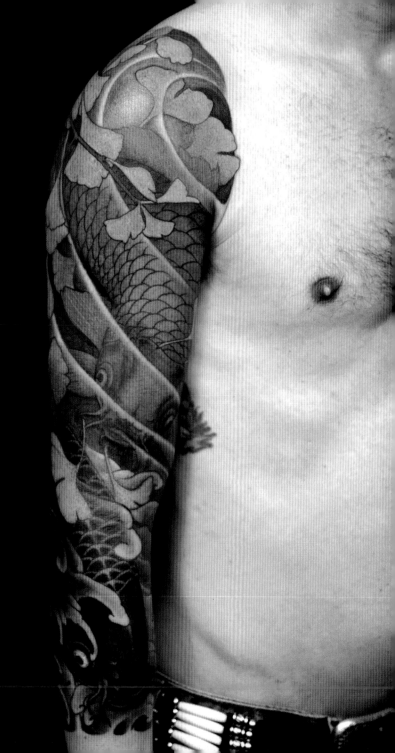

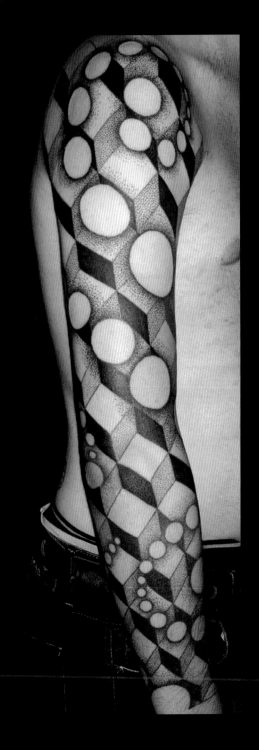

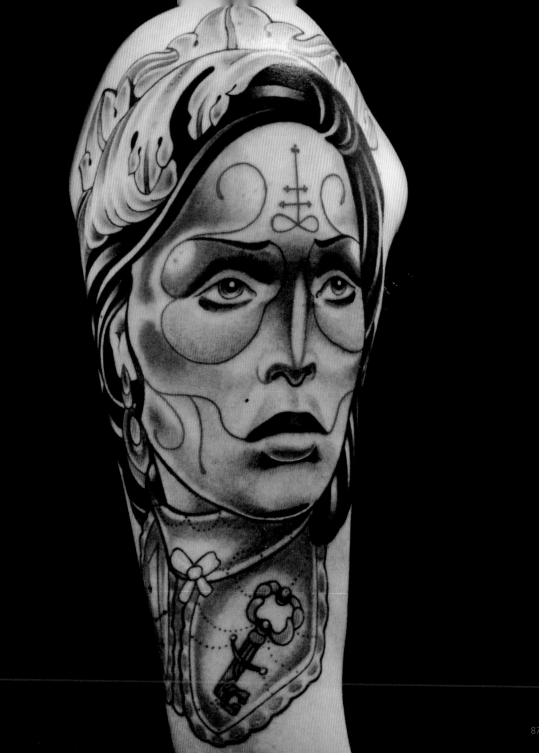

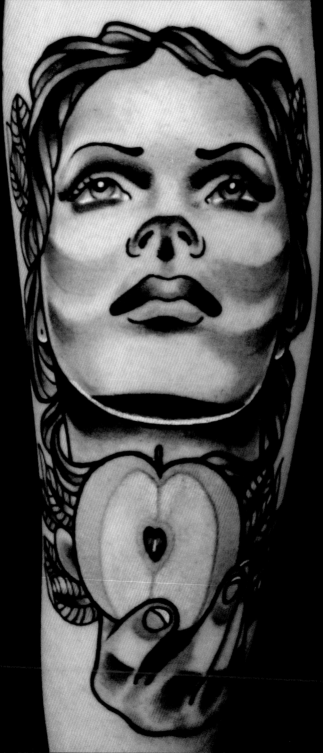

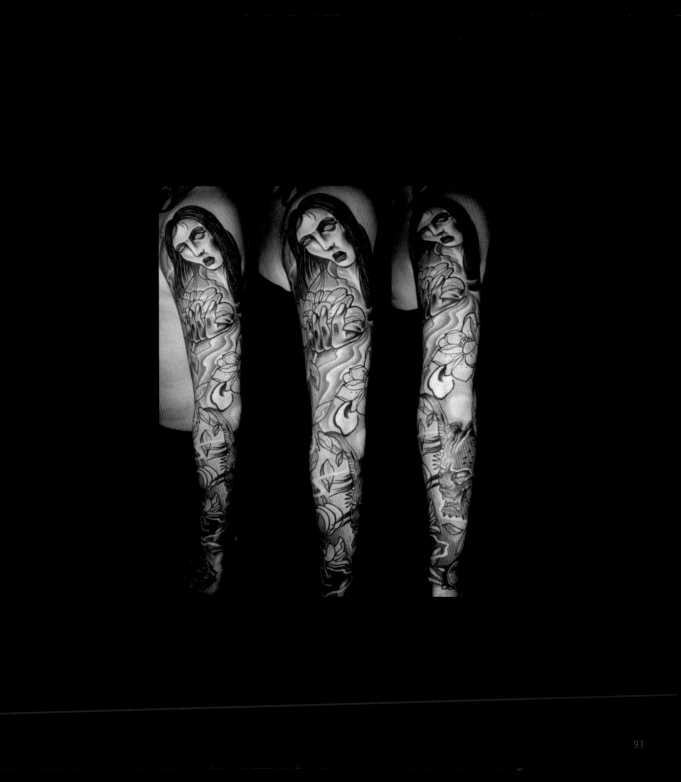

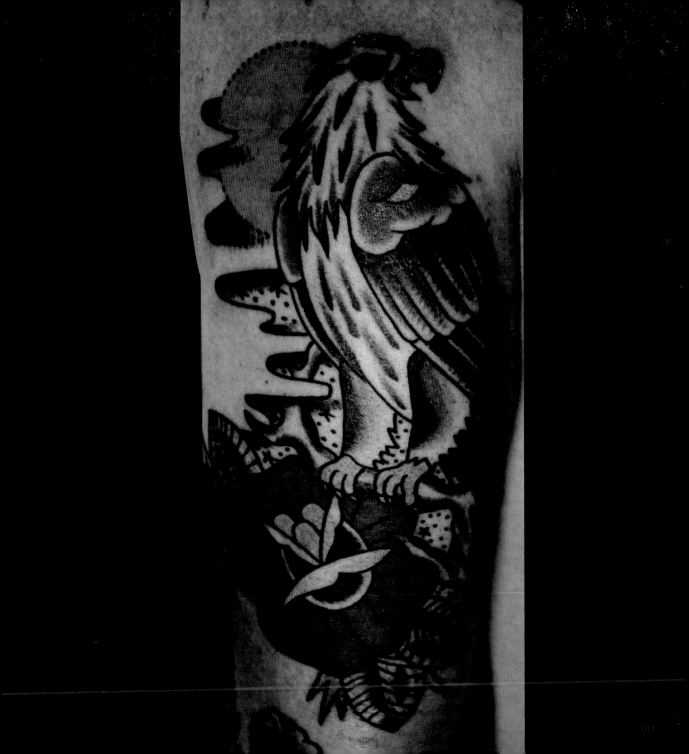

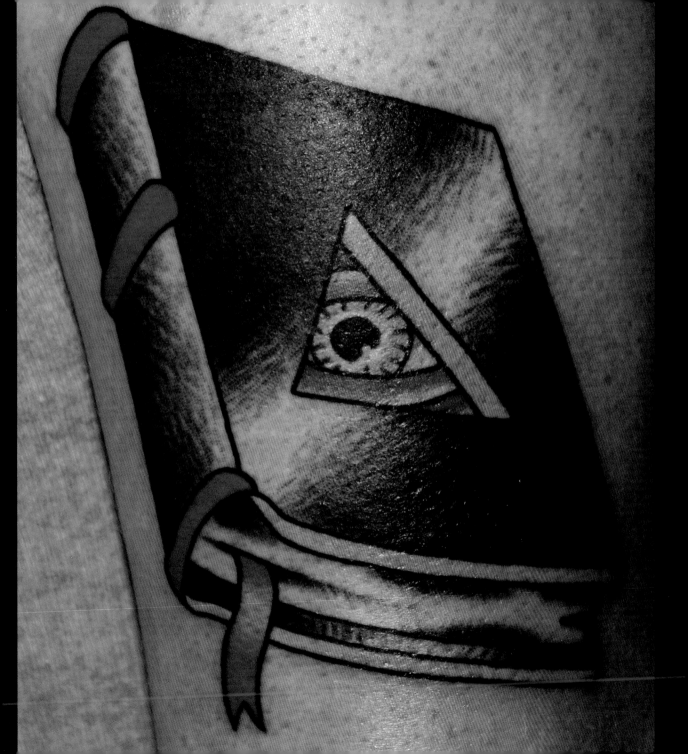

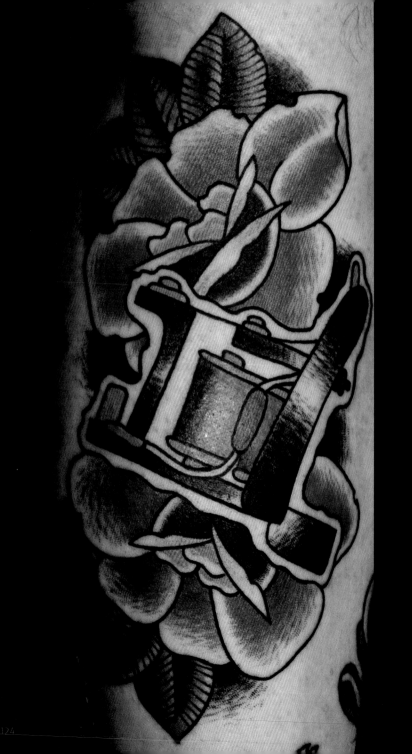
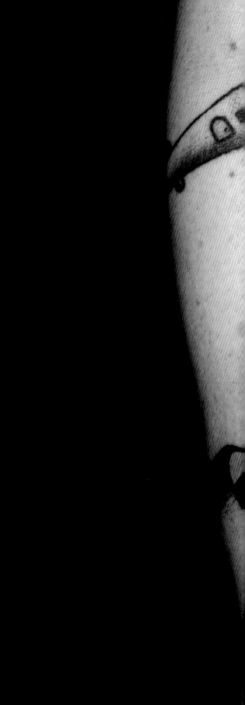

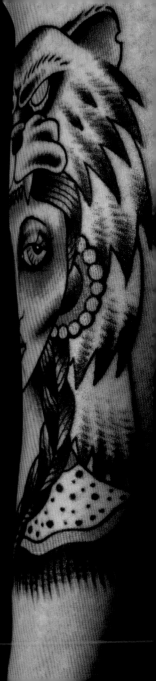

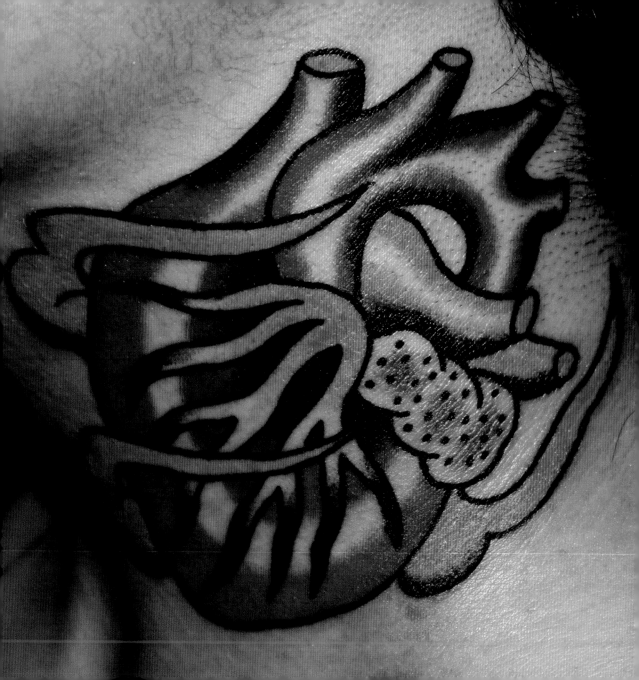

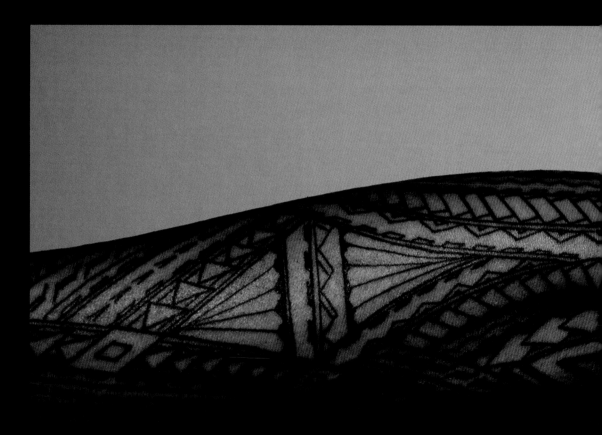

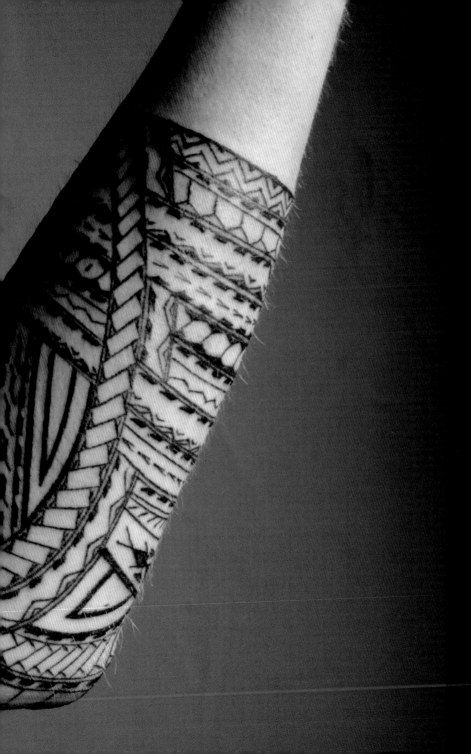

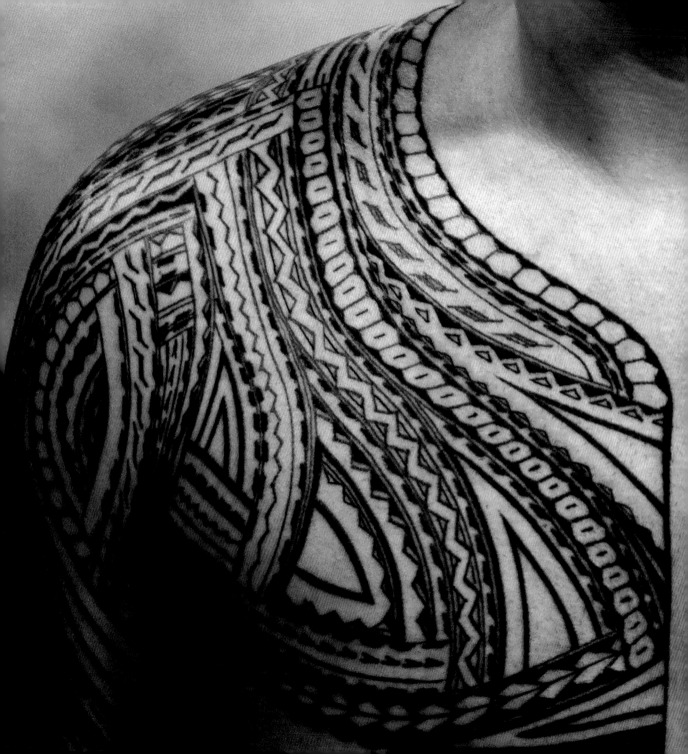

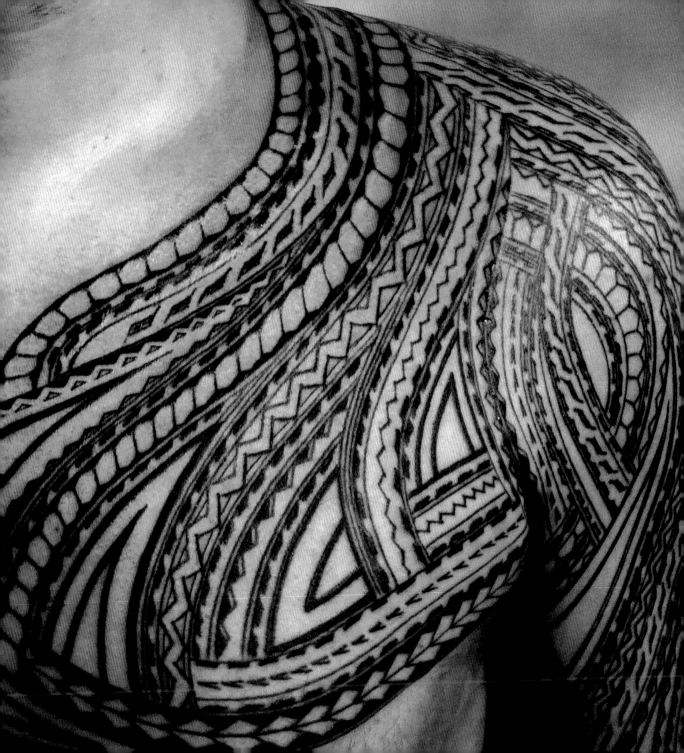

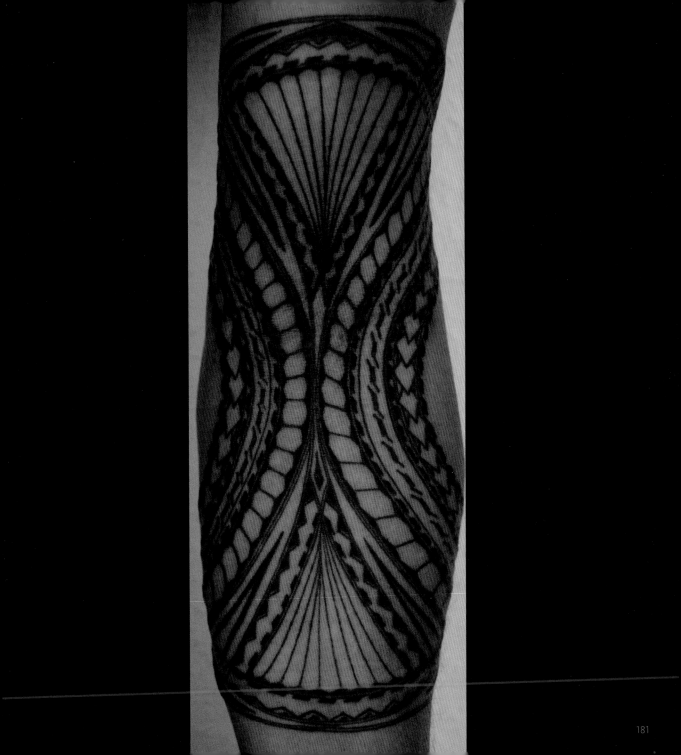

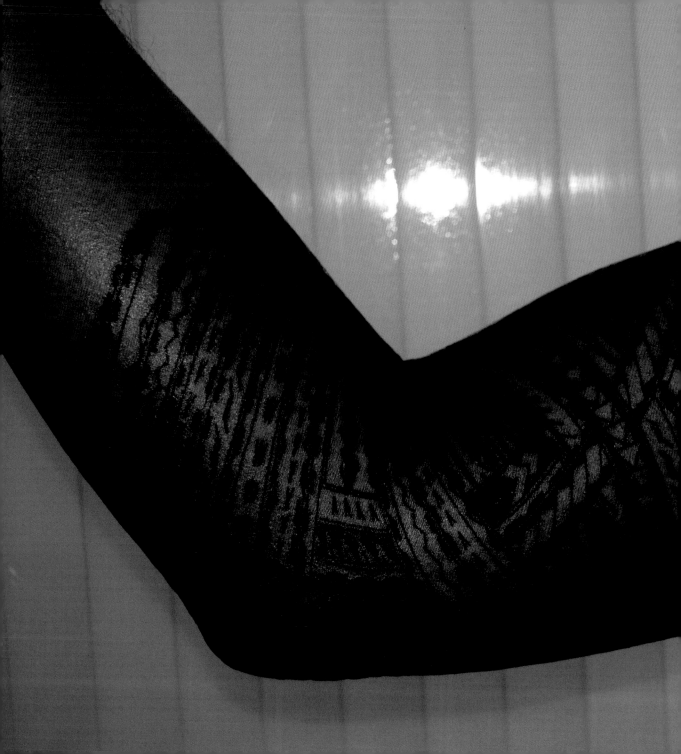

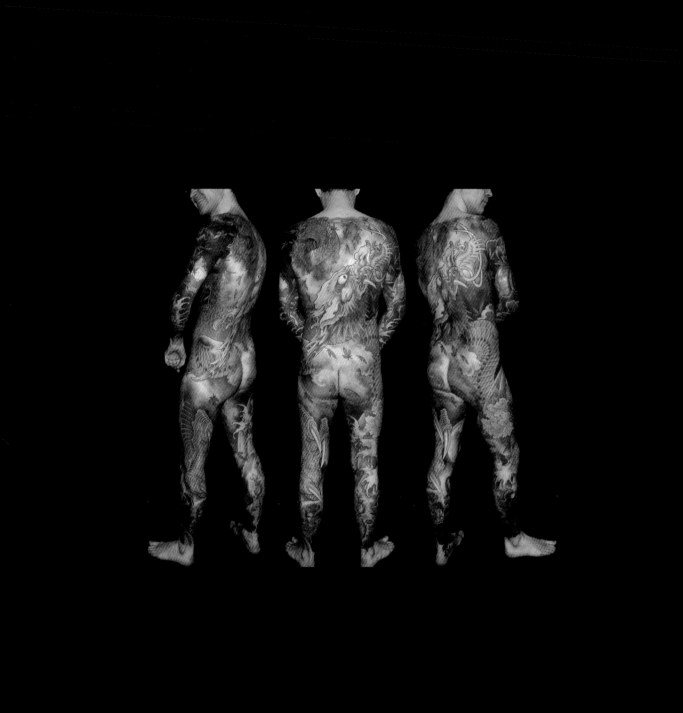

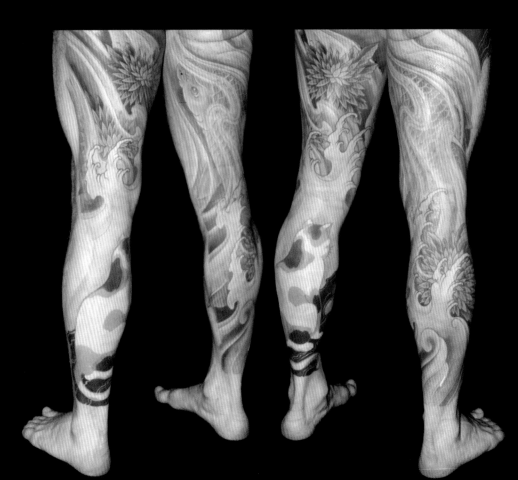

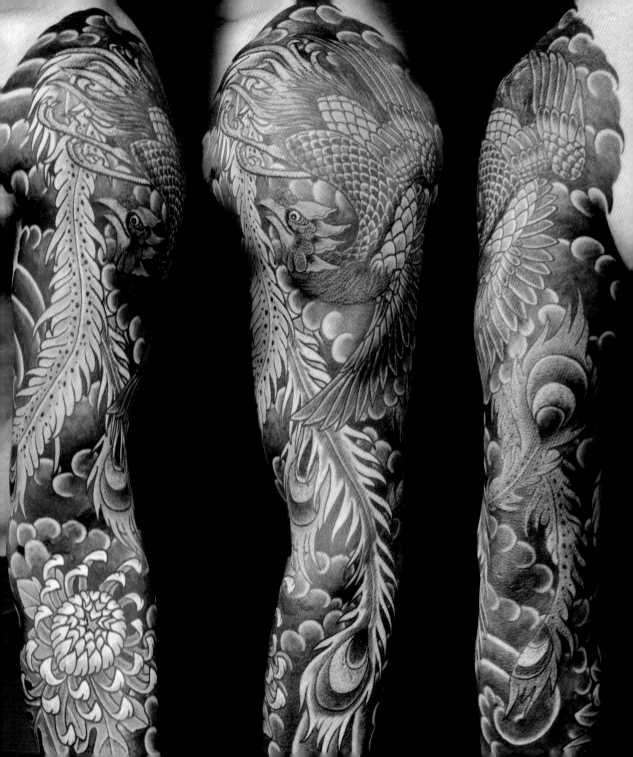

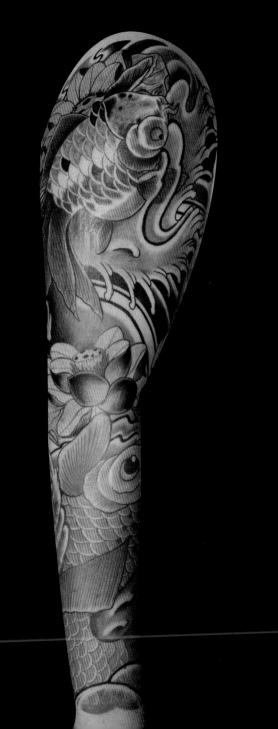

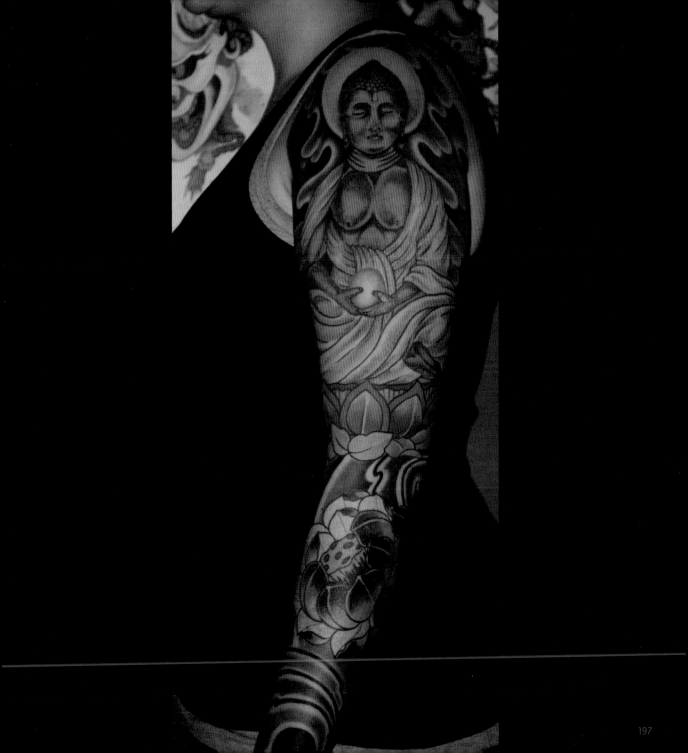

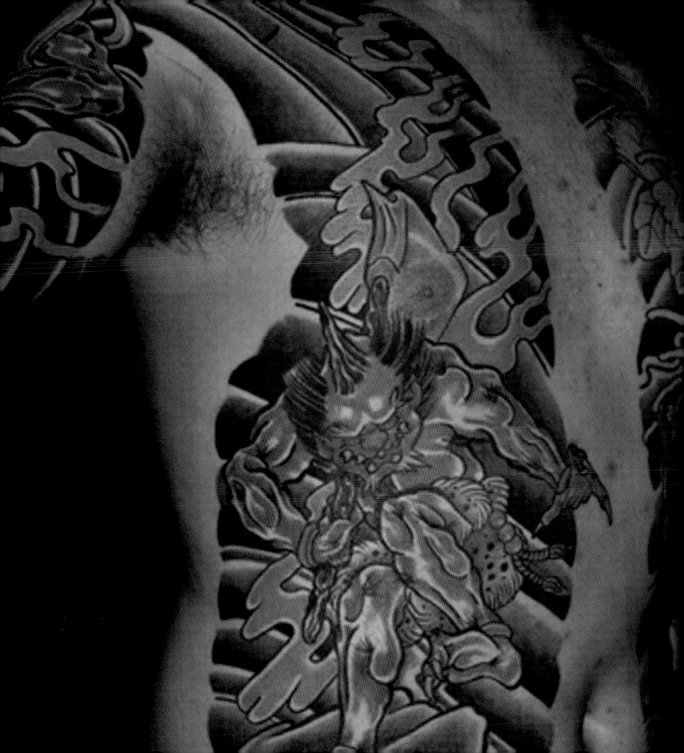

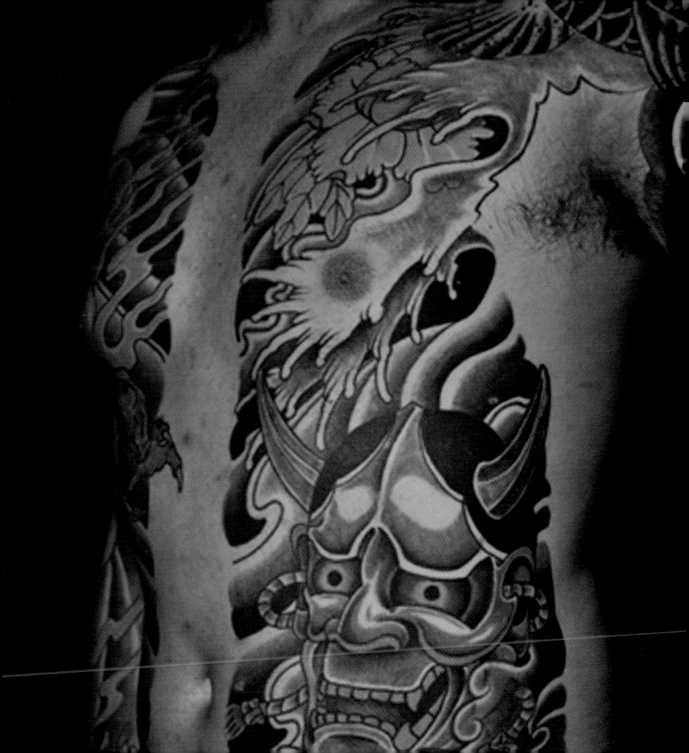

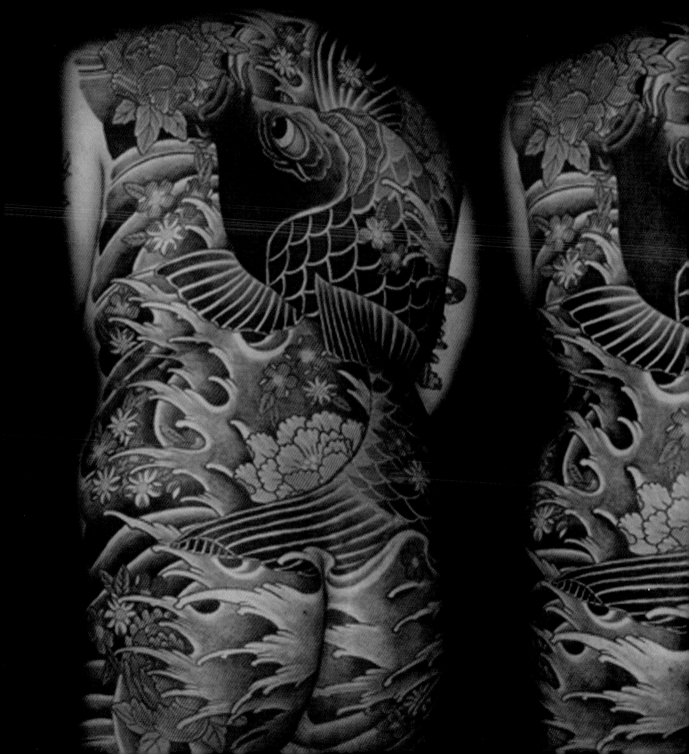

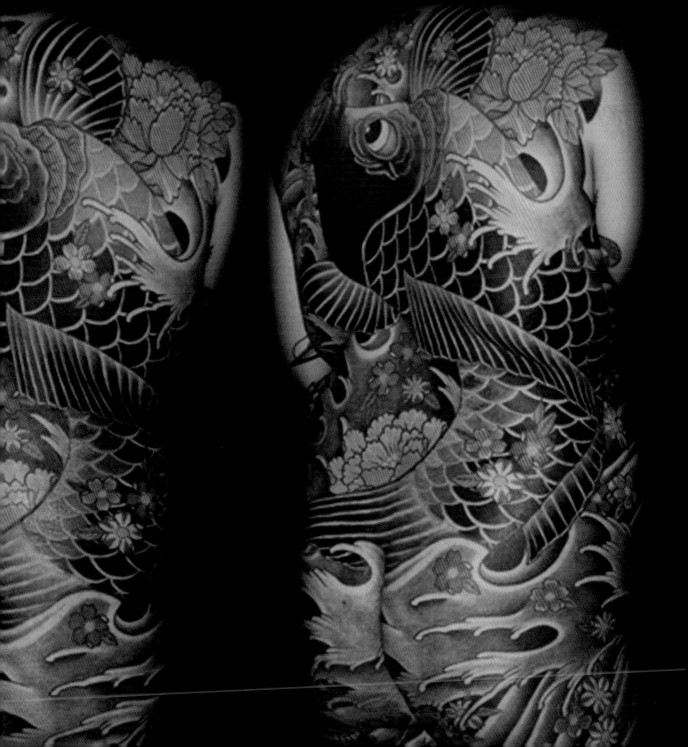

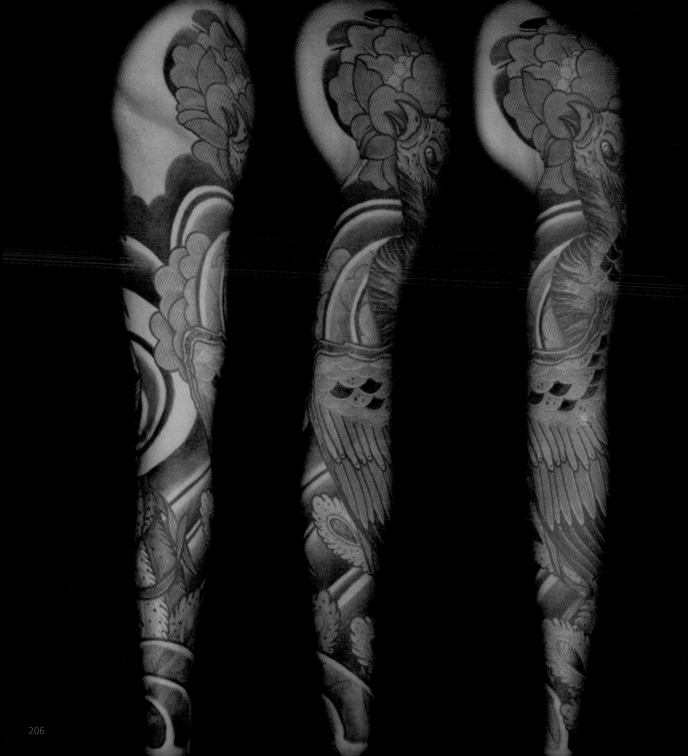

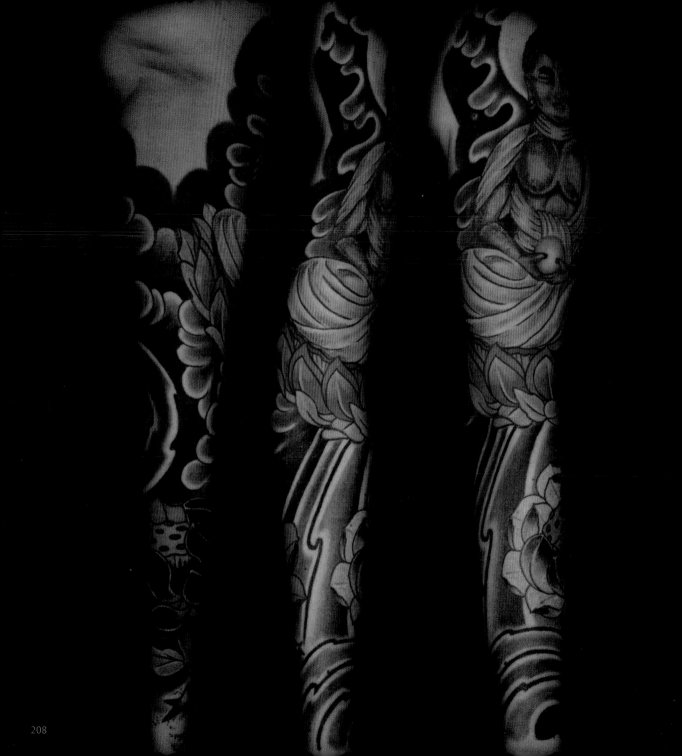

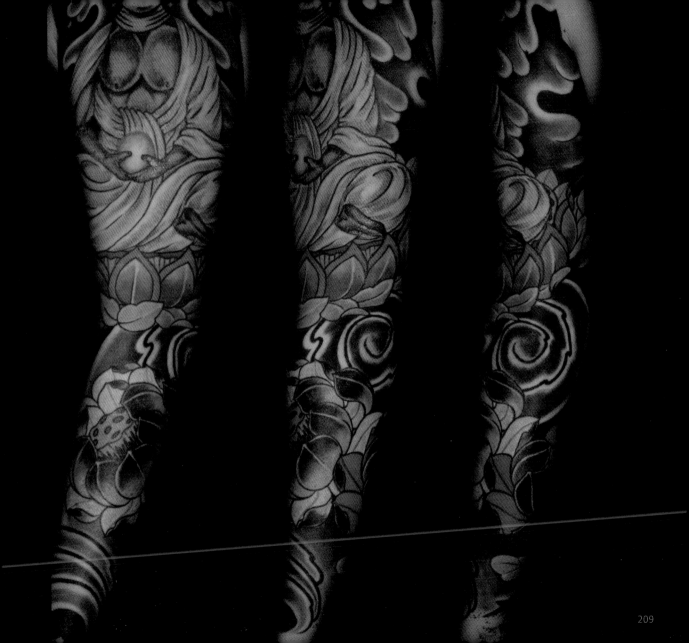

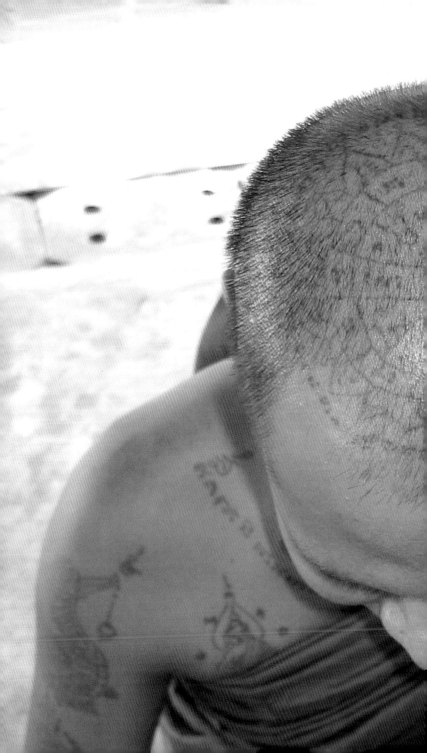

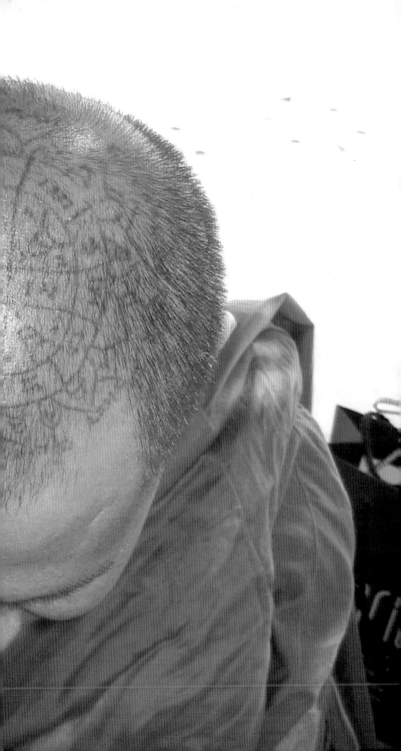

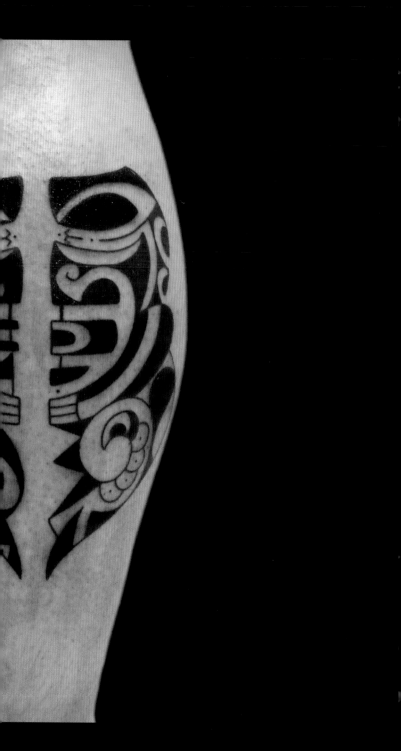

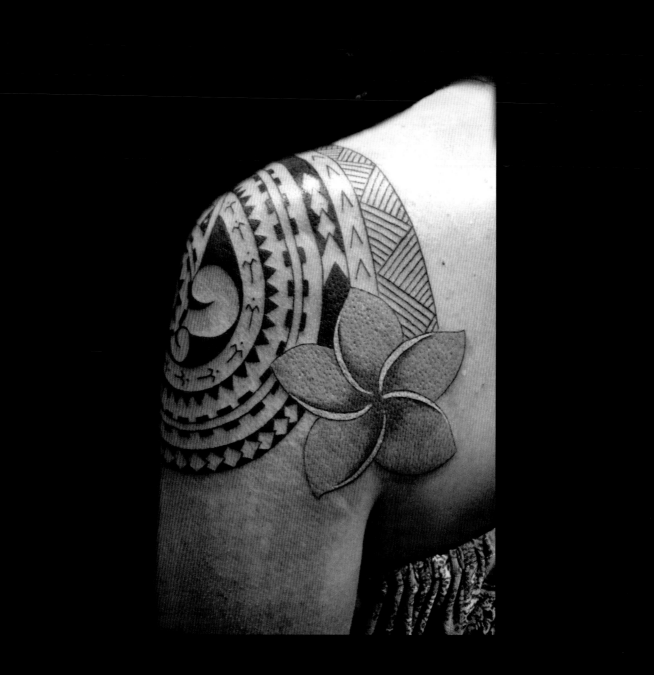

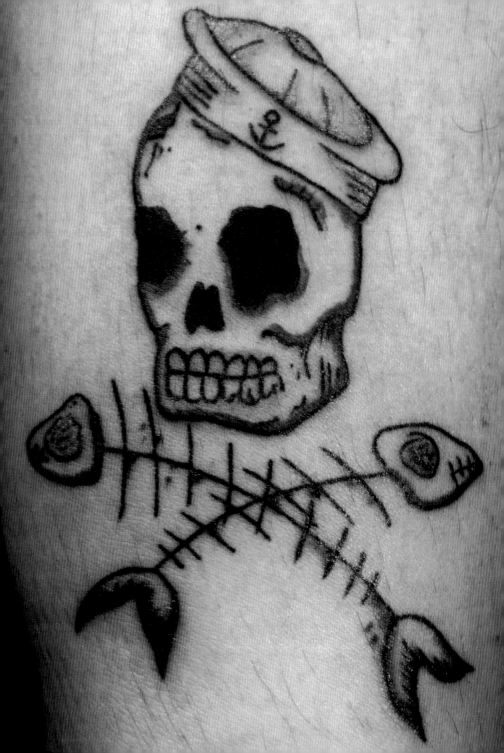

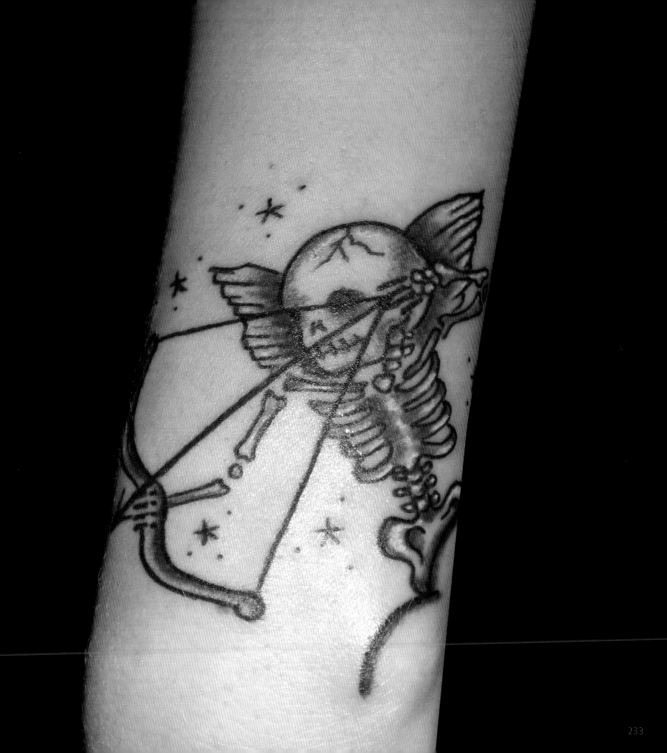

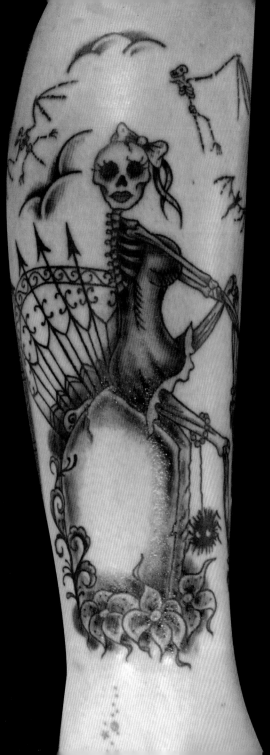
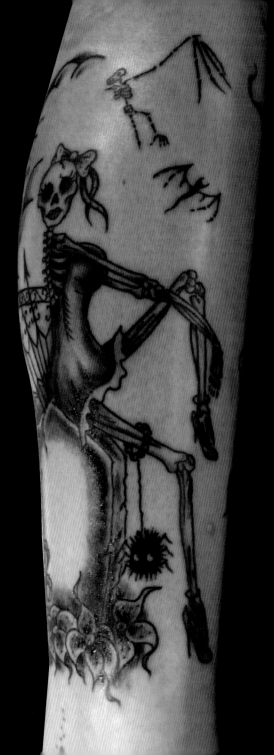

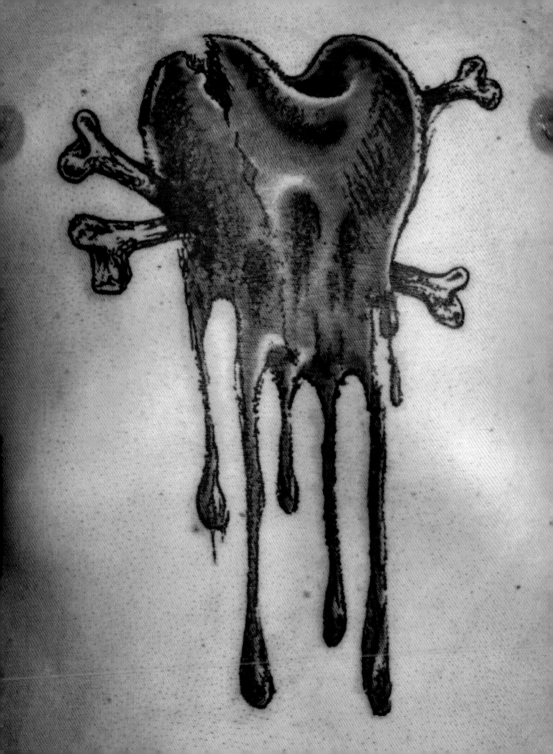

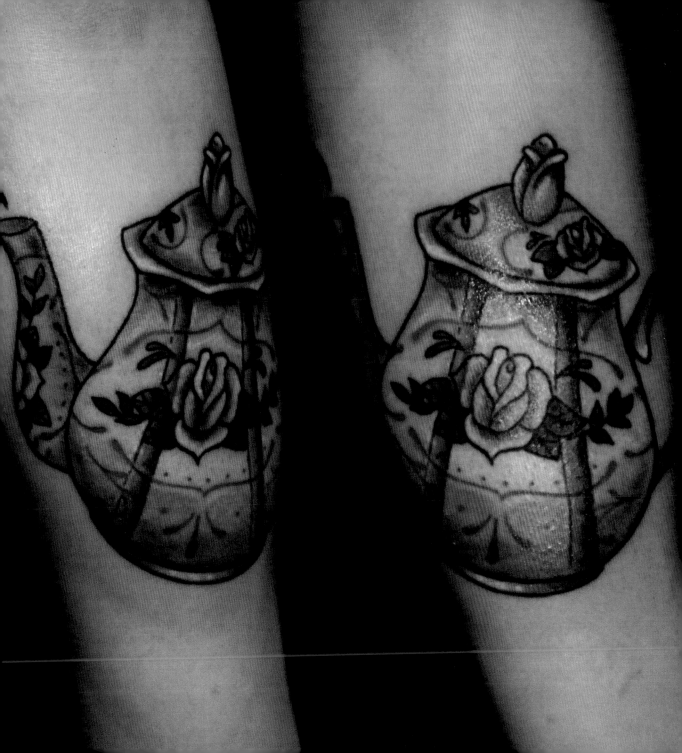

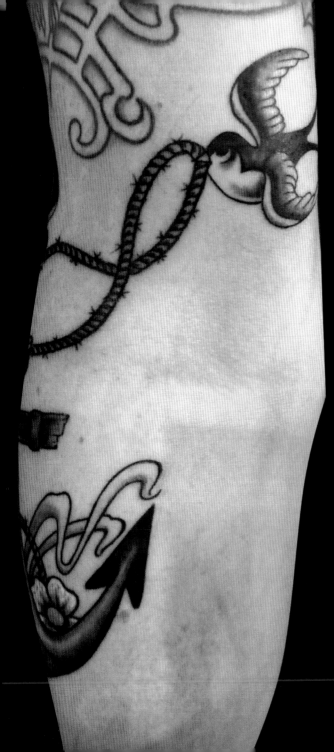

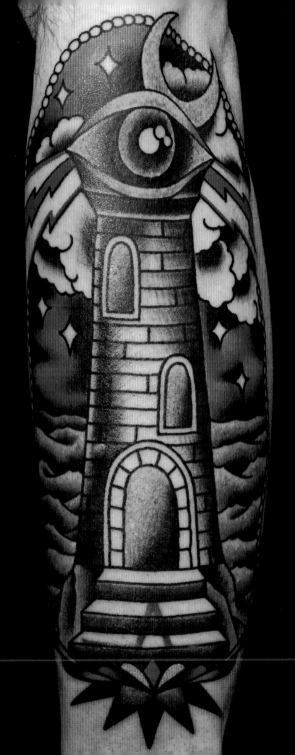

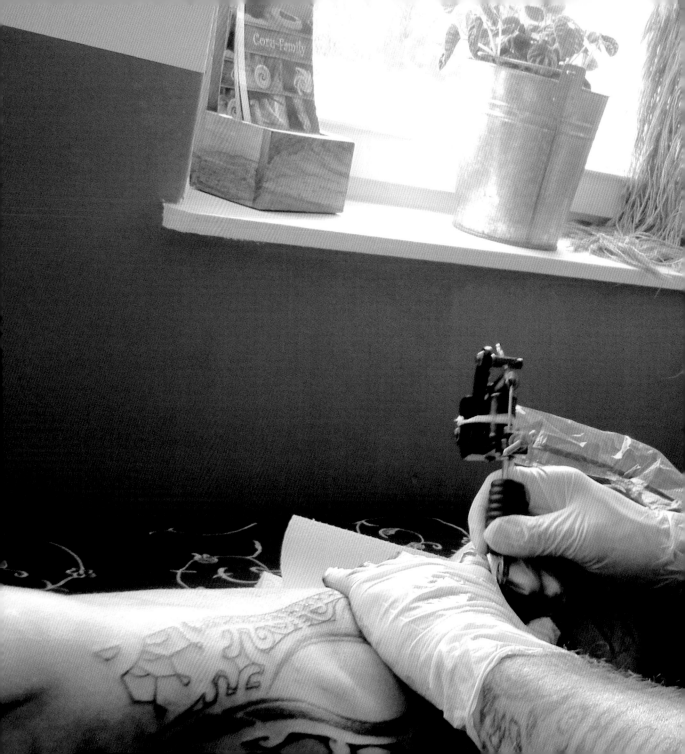

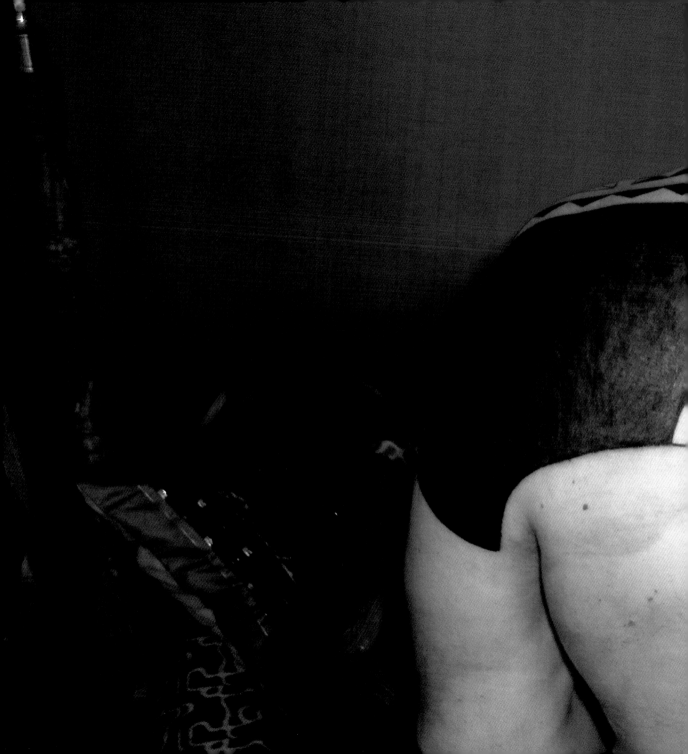

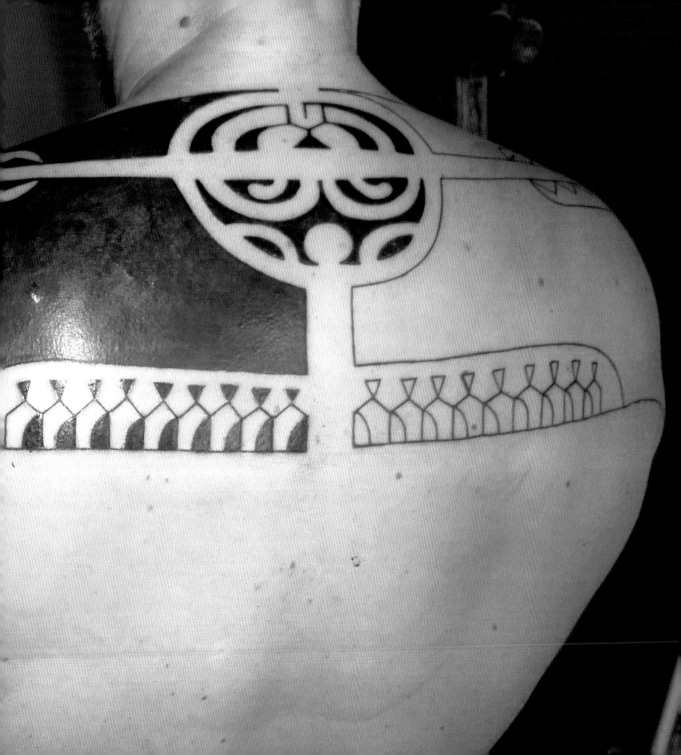

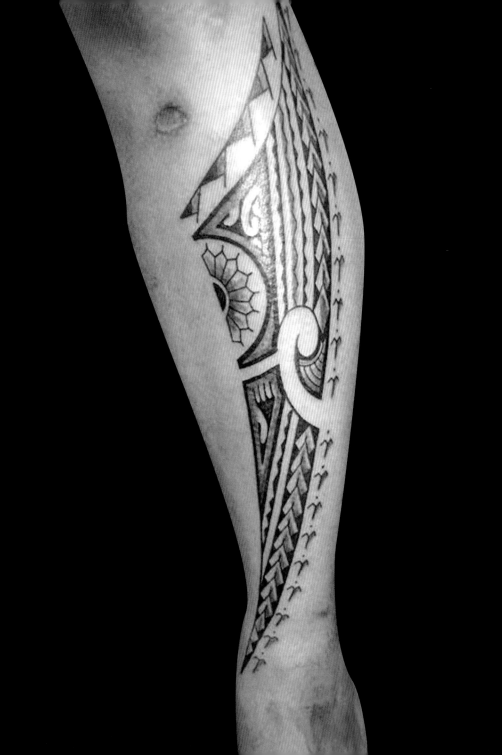

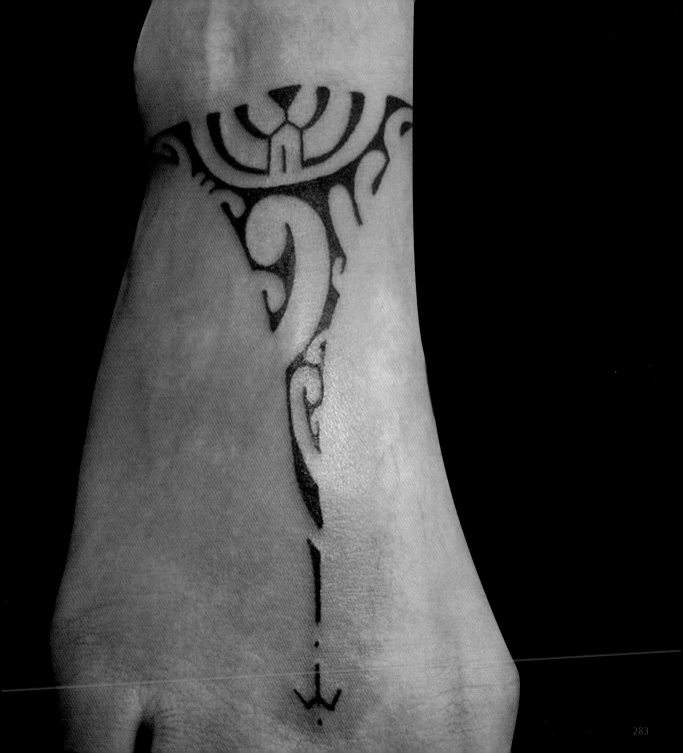

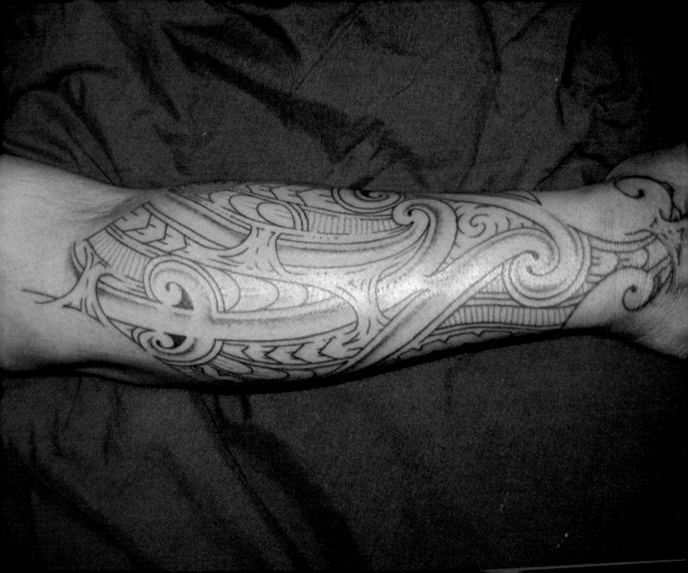

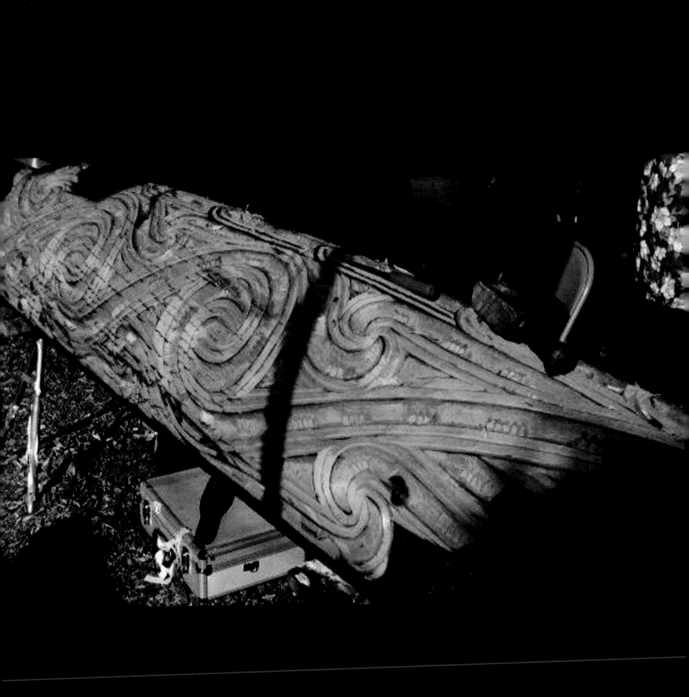

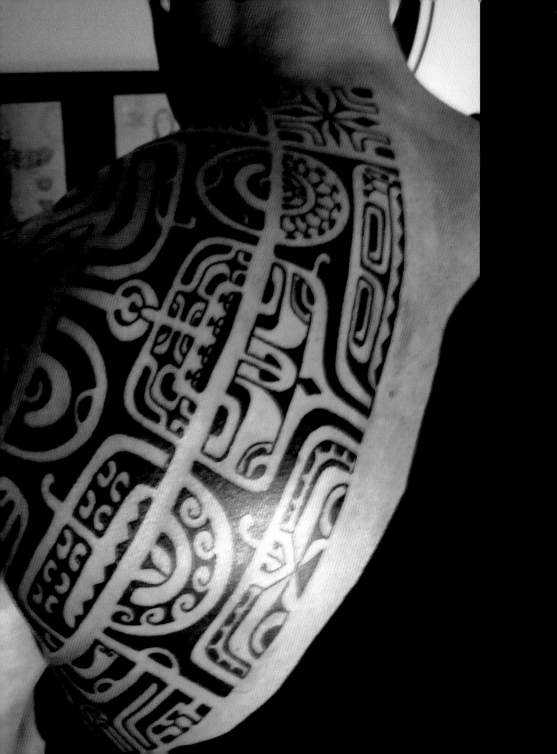

Throwing and concept by Soline Penion, patterns by Po'oino Yrondi

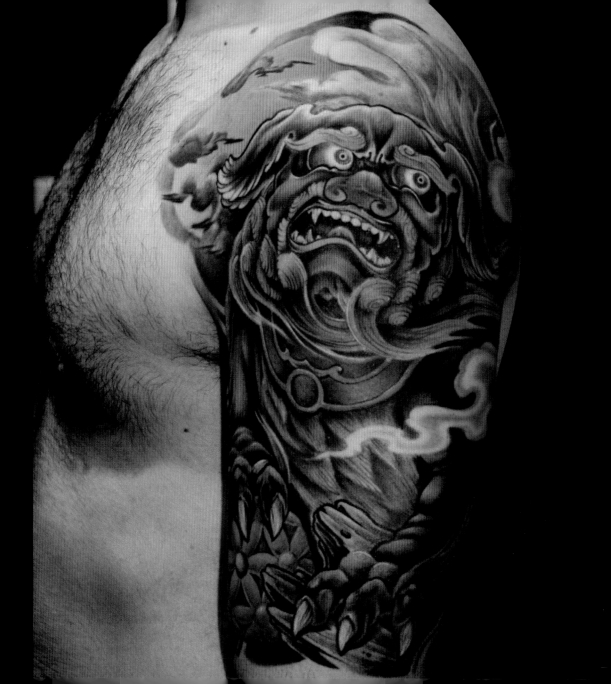

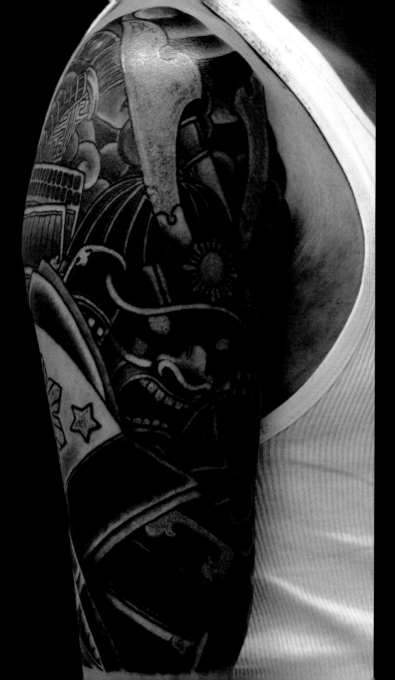

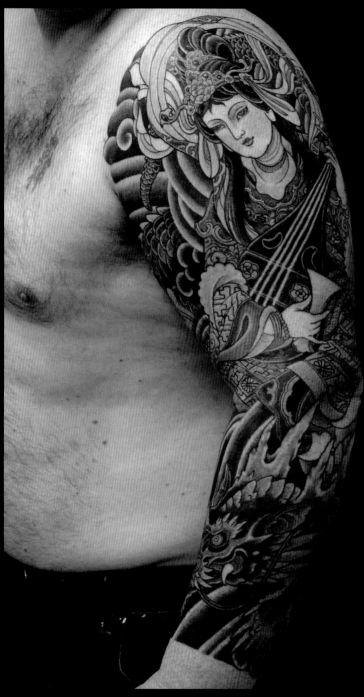

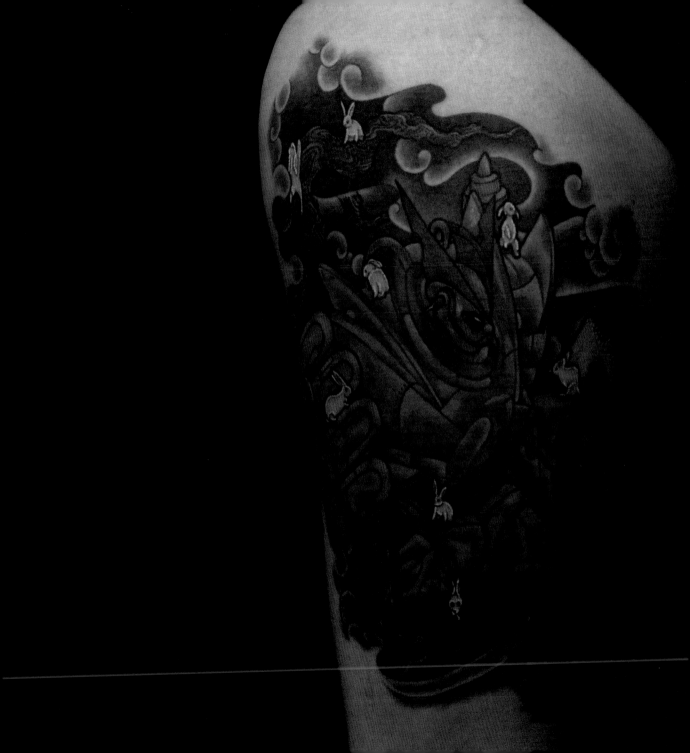

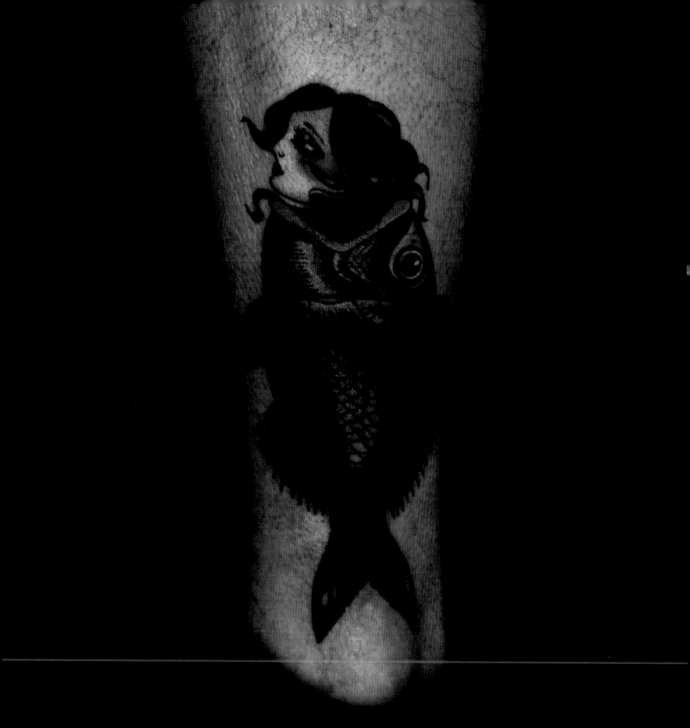

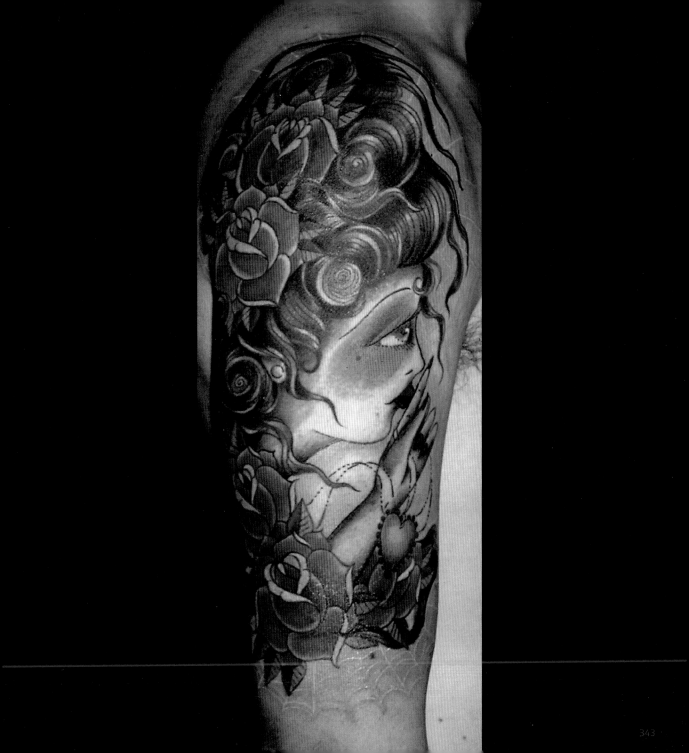

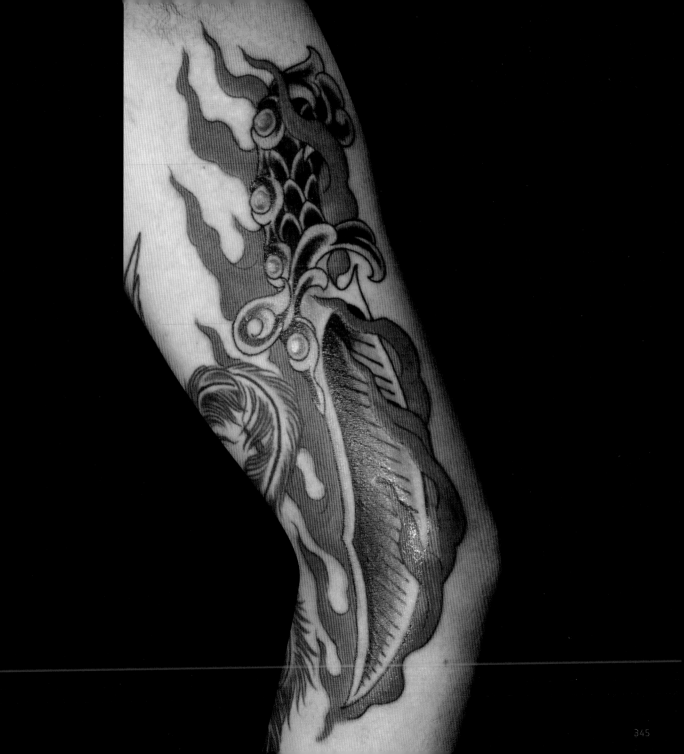

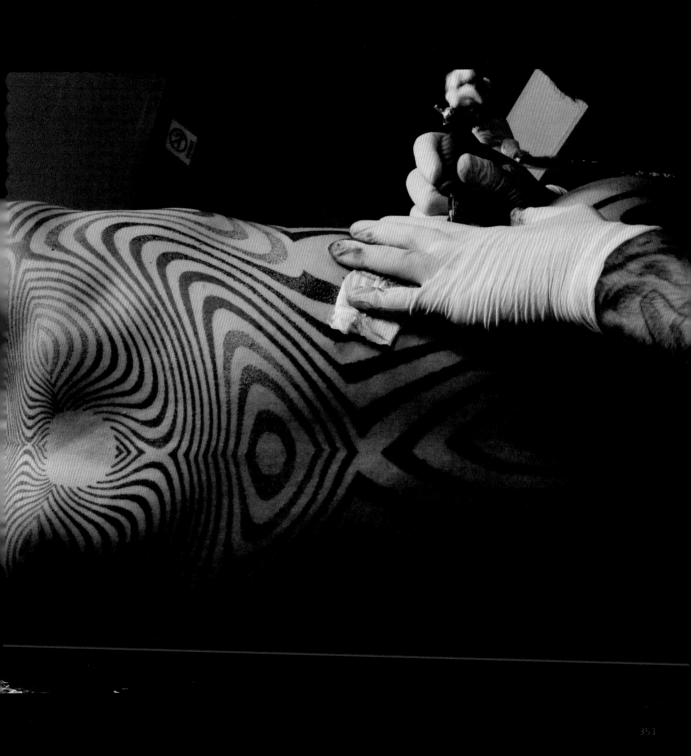

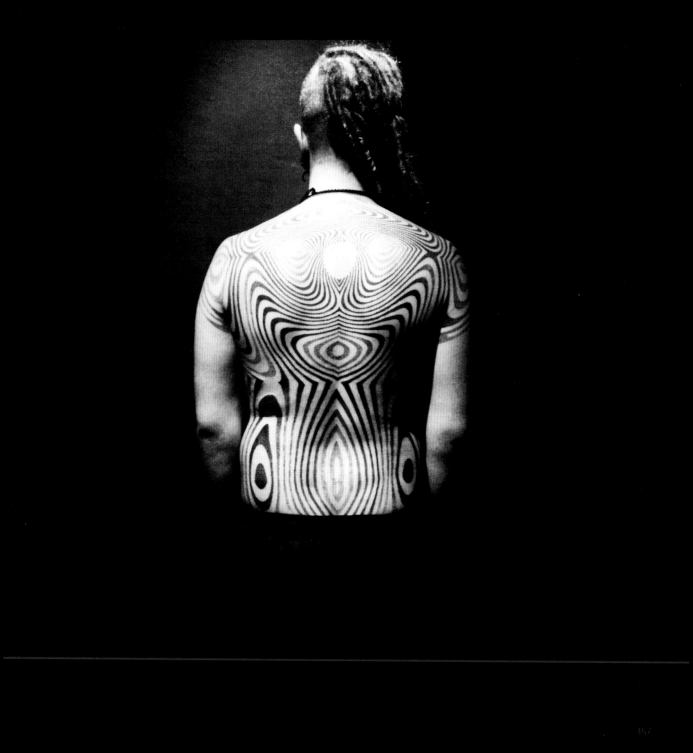

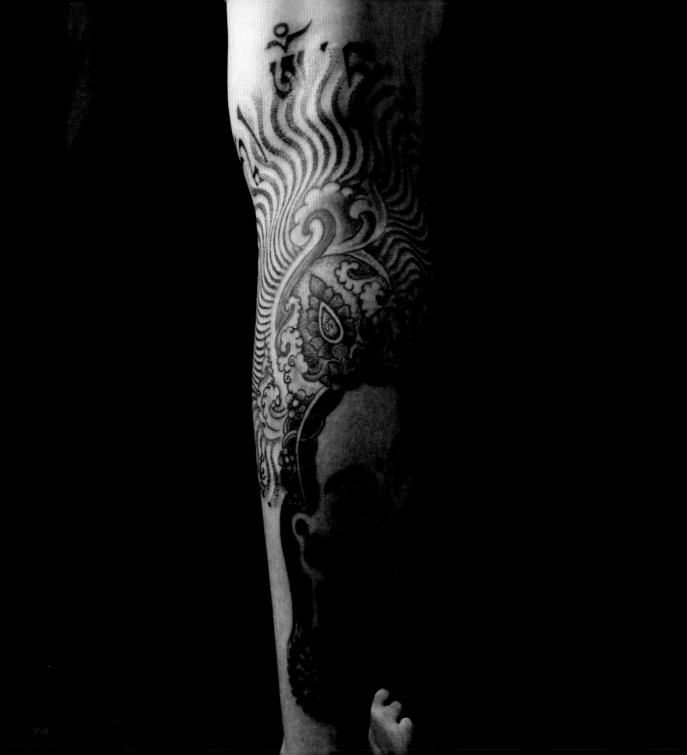

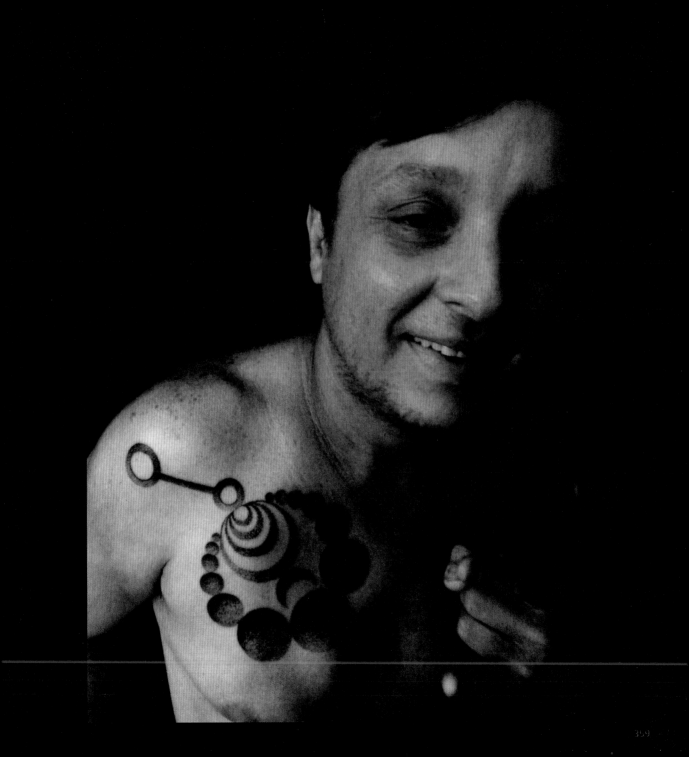

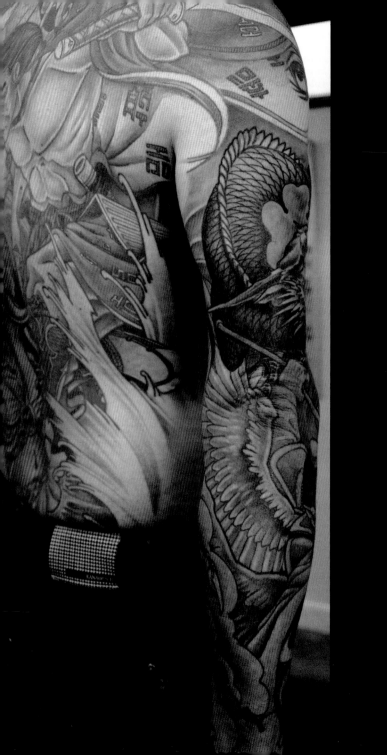

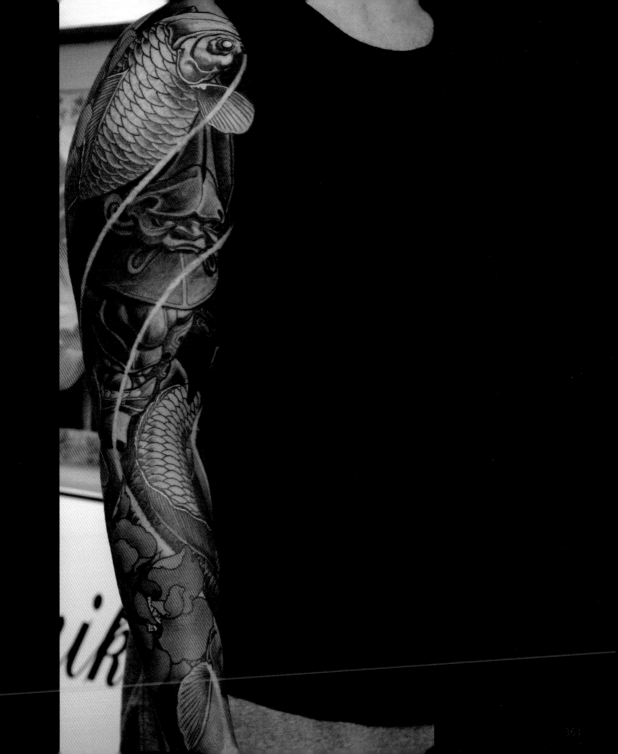

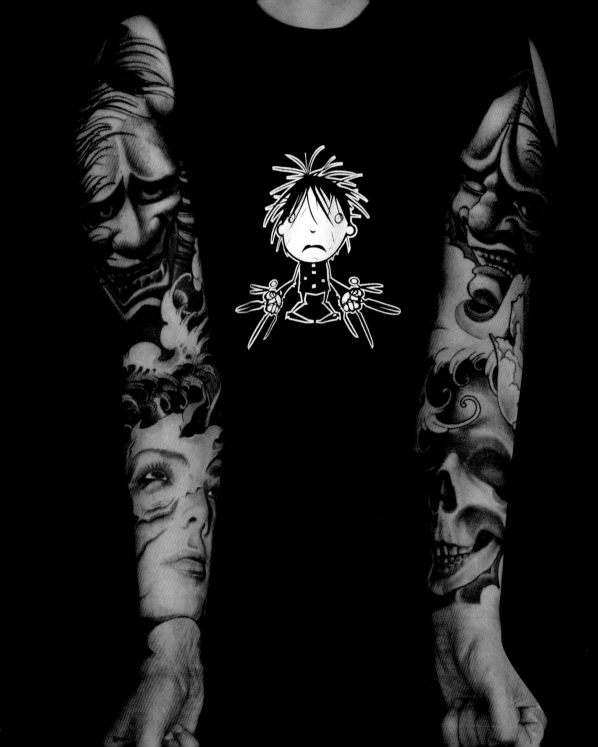

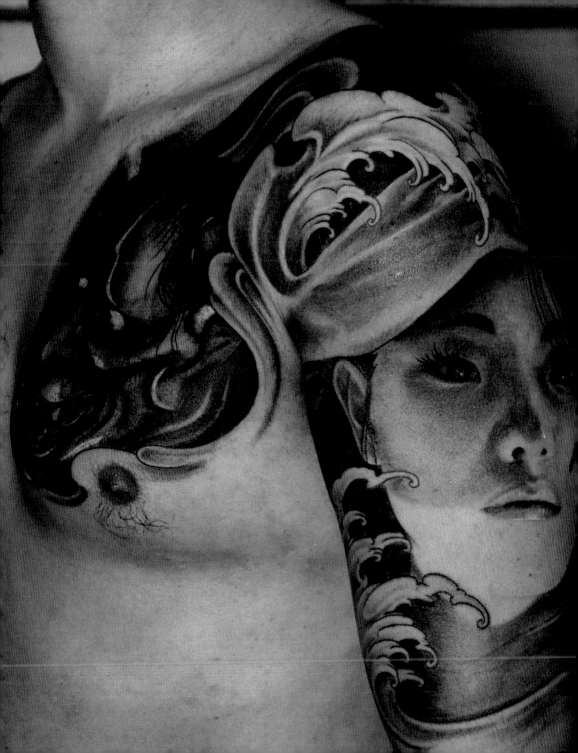

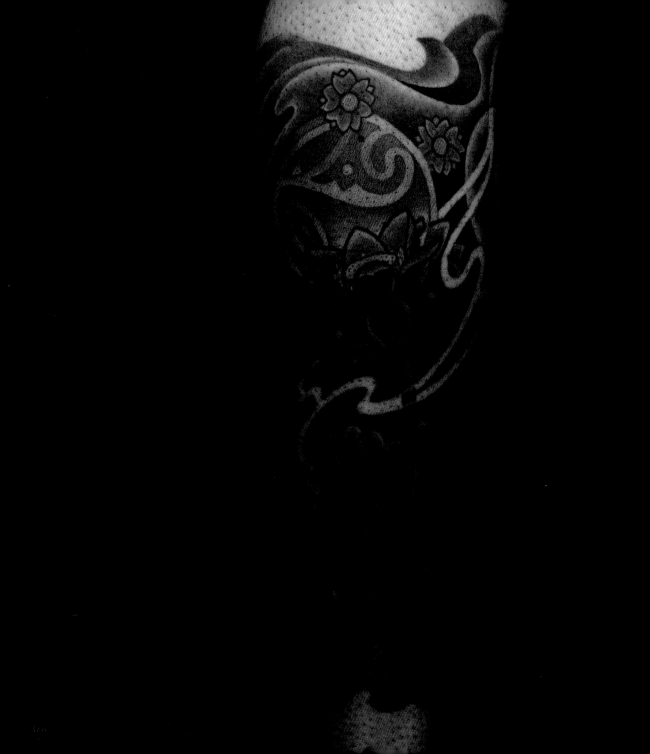

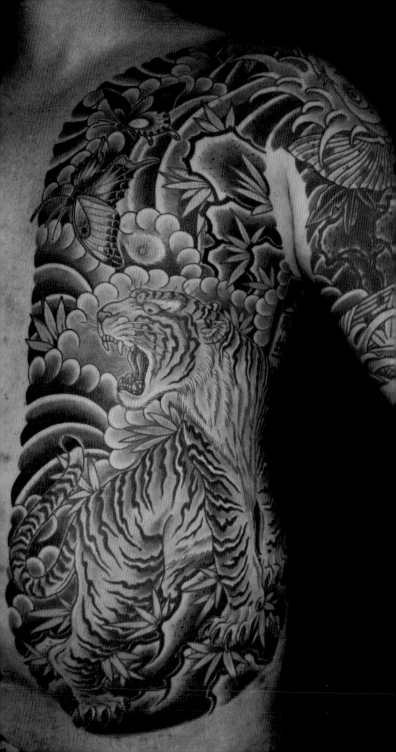

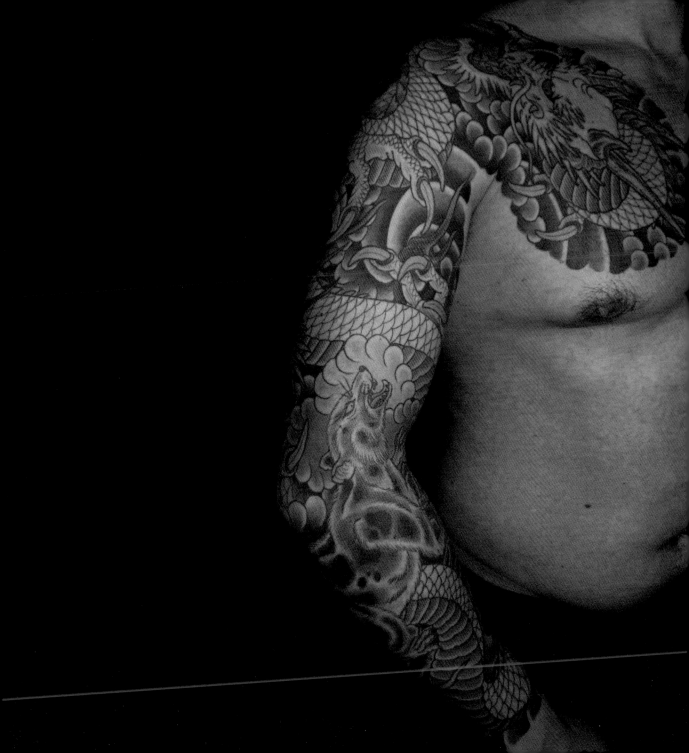

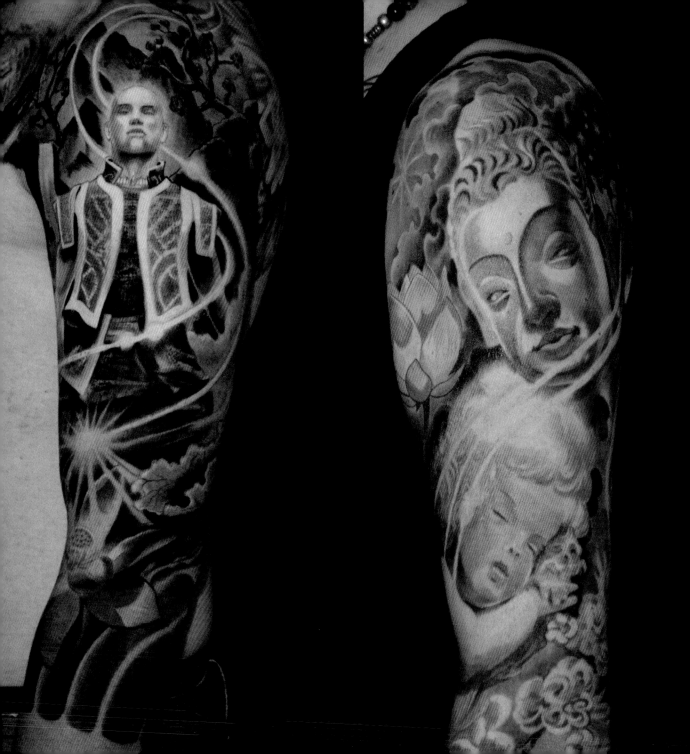

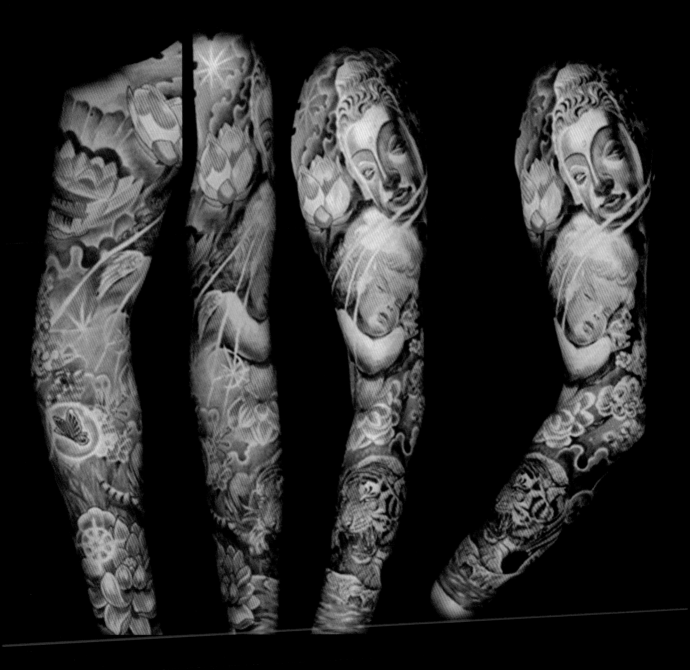

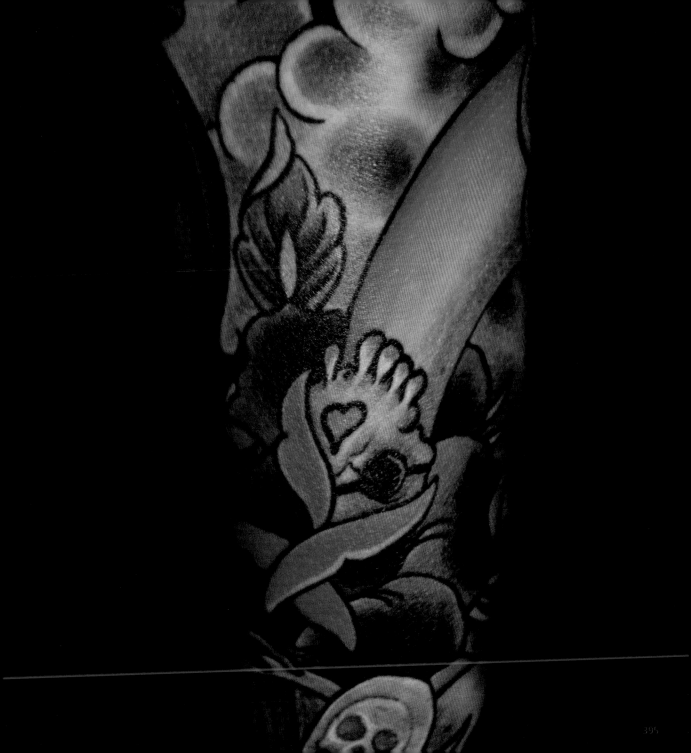

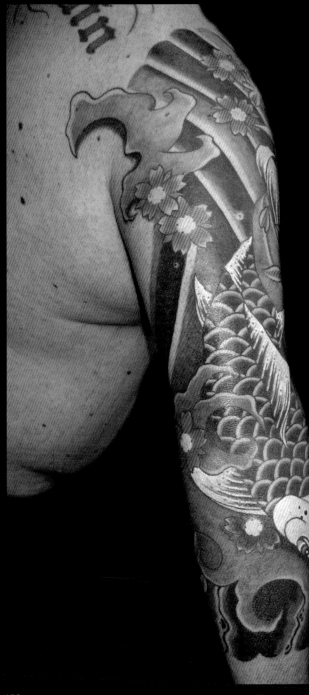

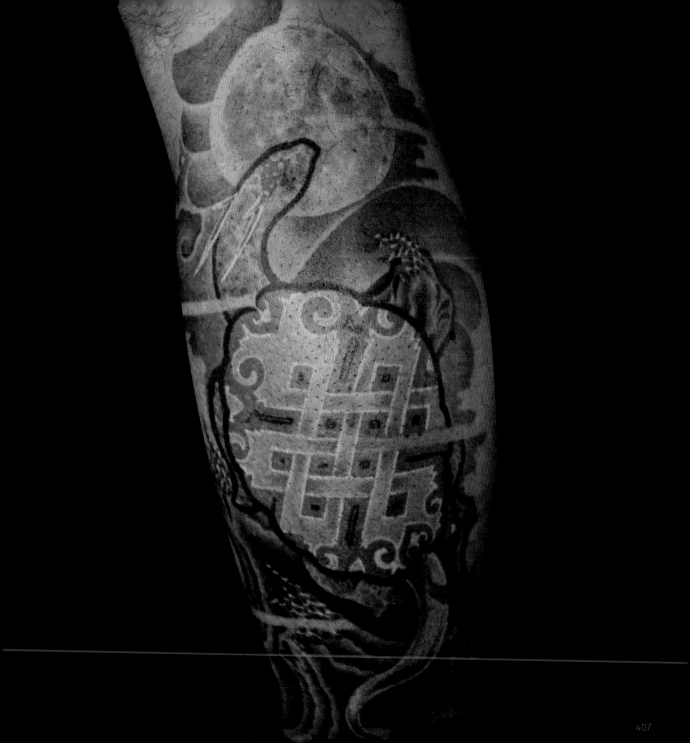

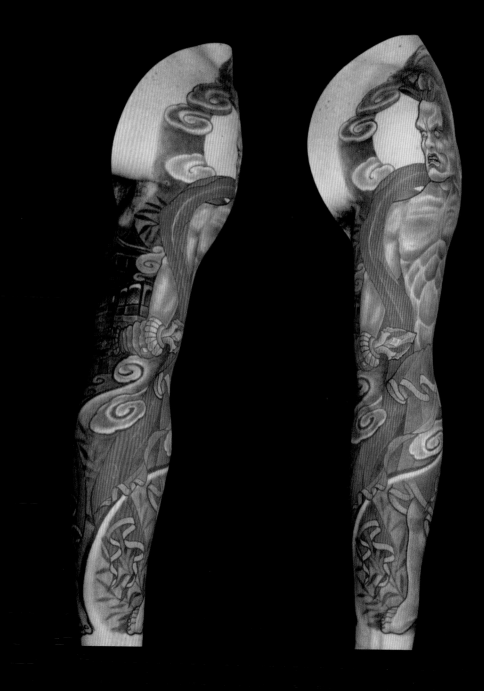

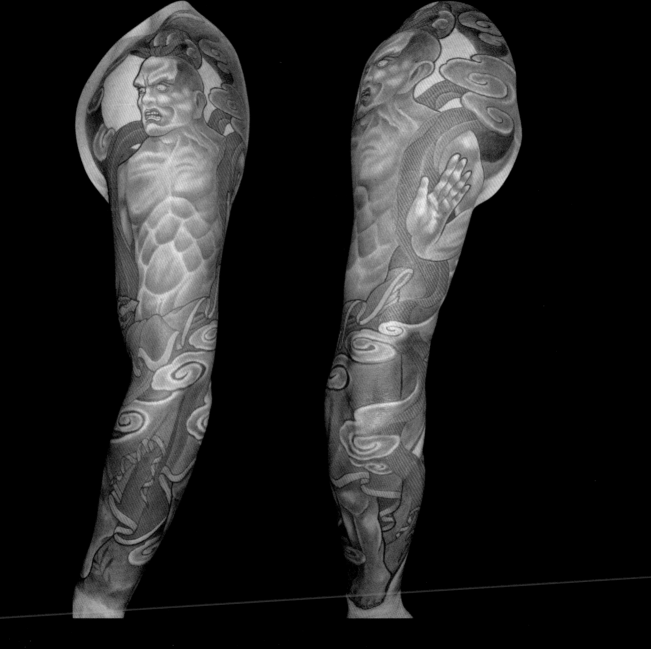

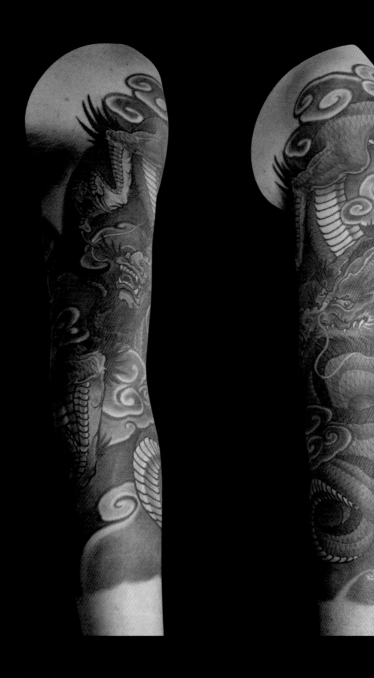

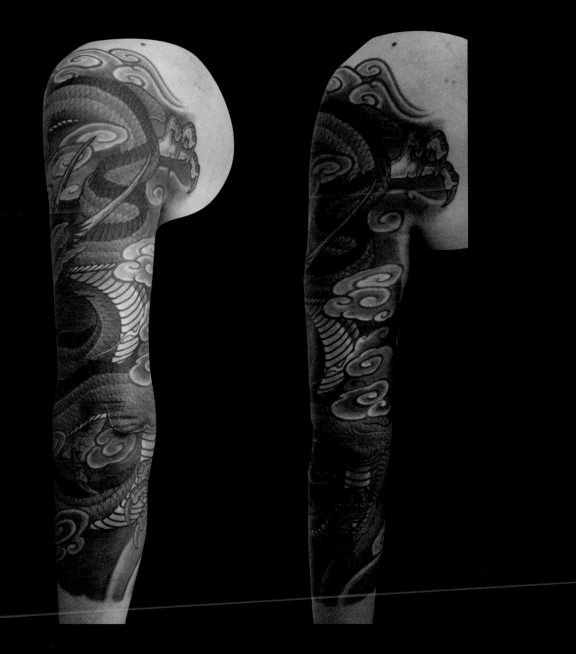

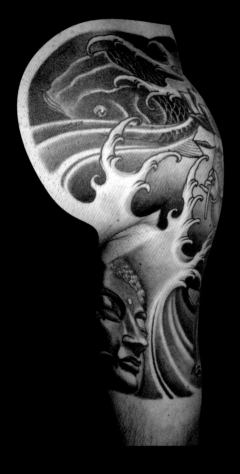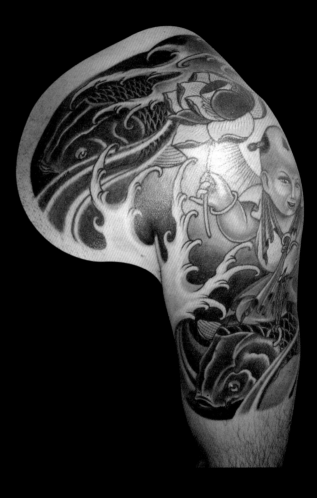

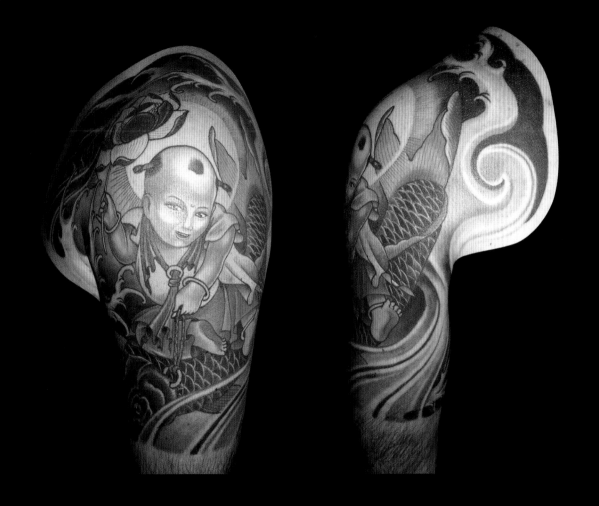

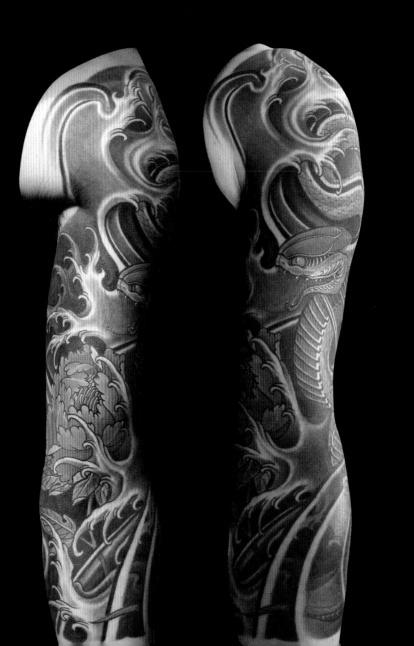

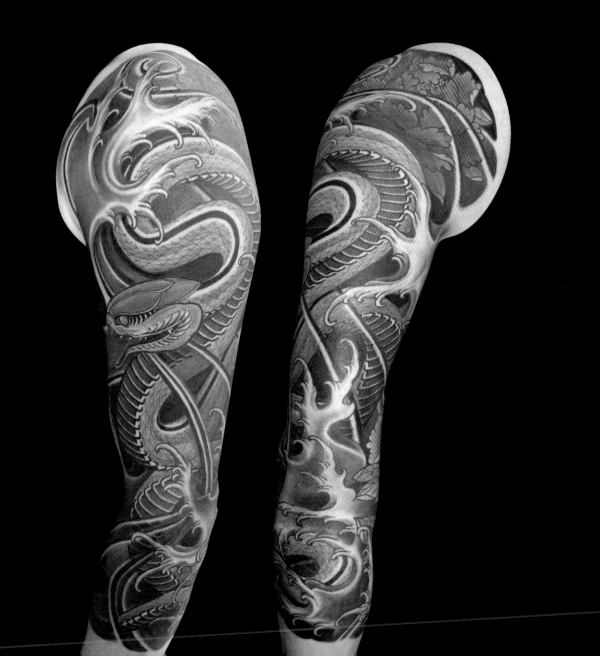

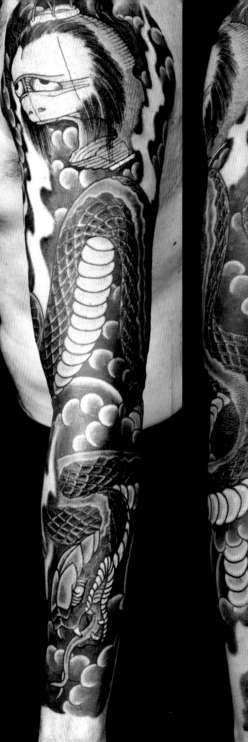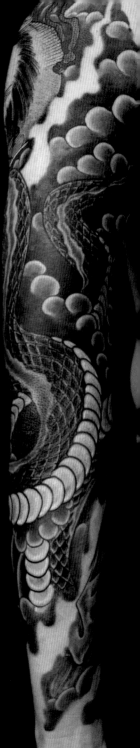

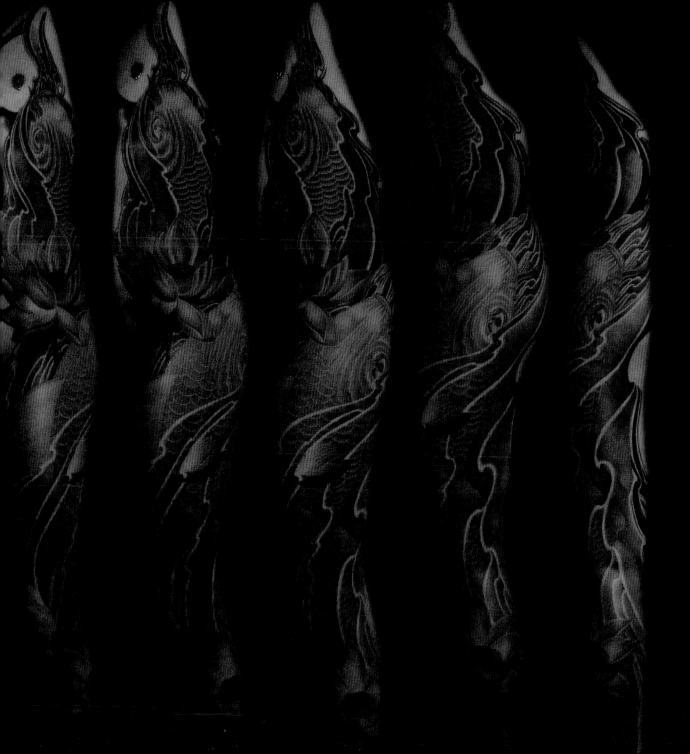

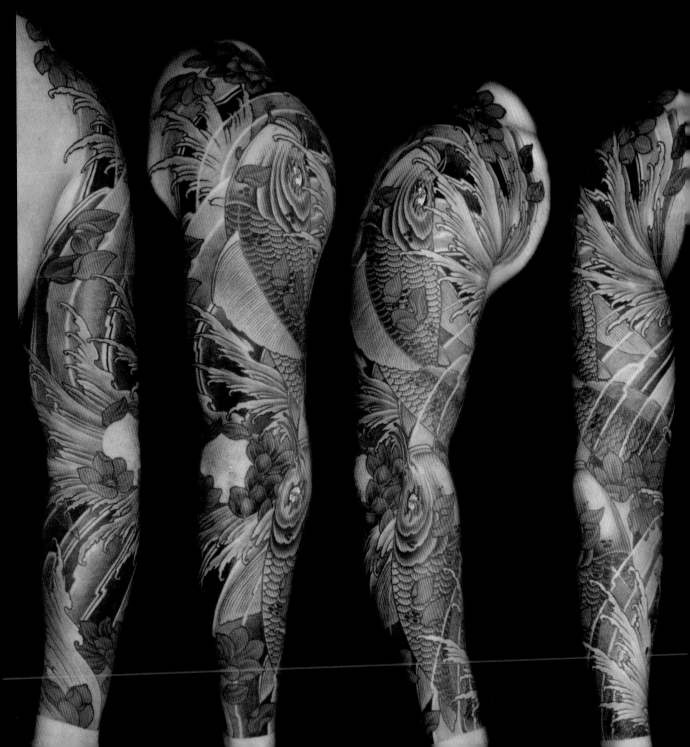

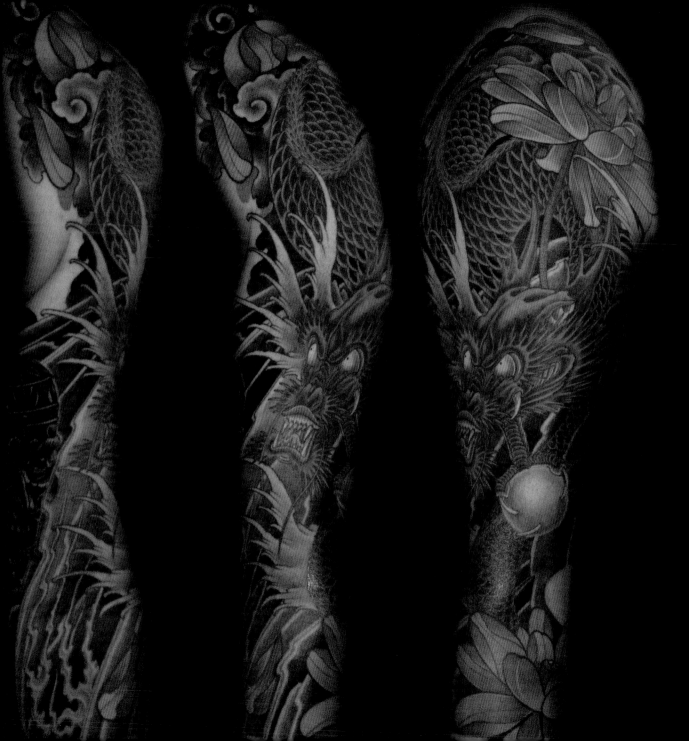

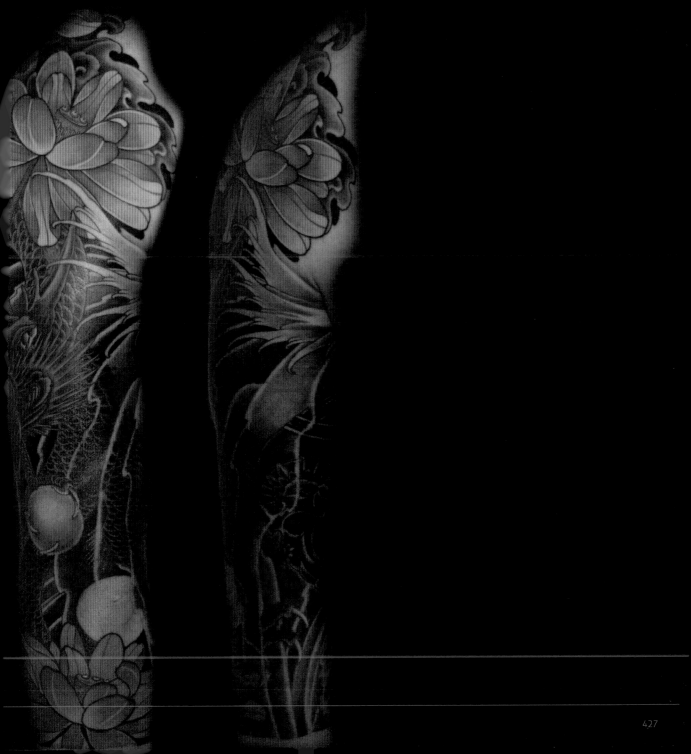

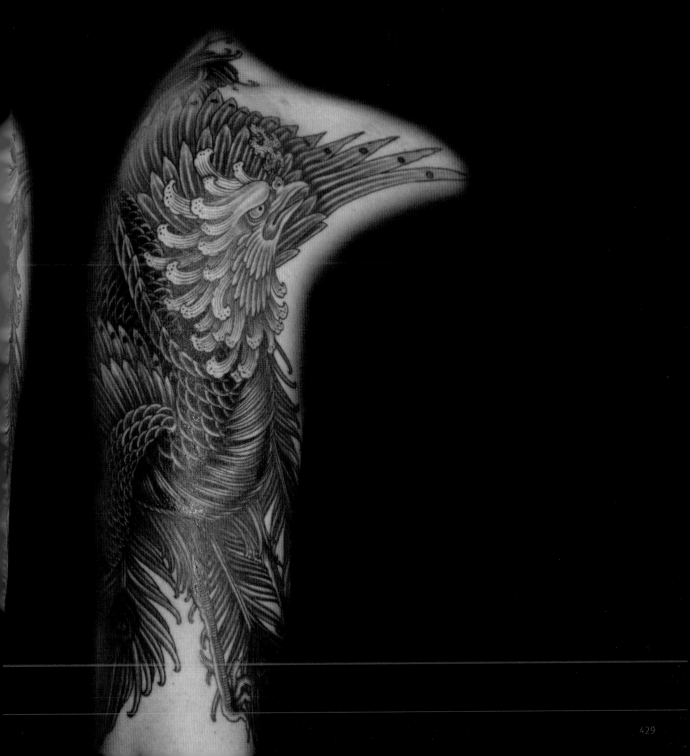

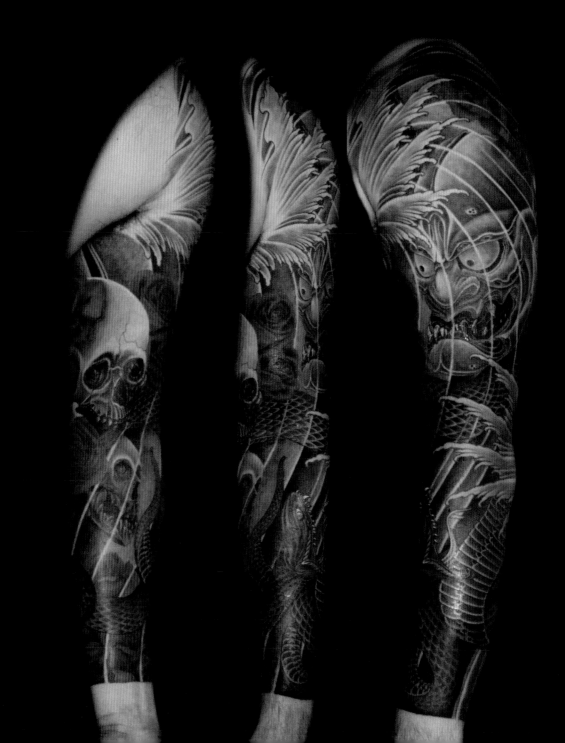

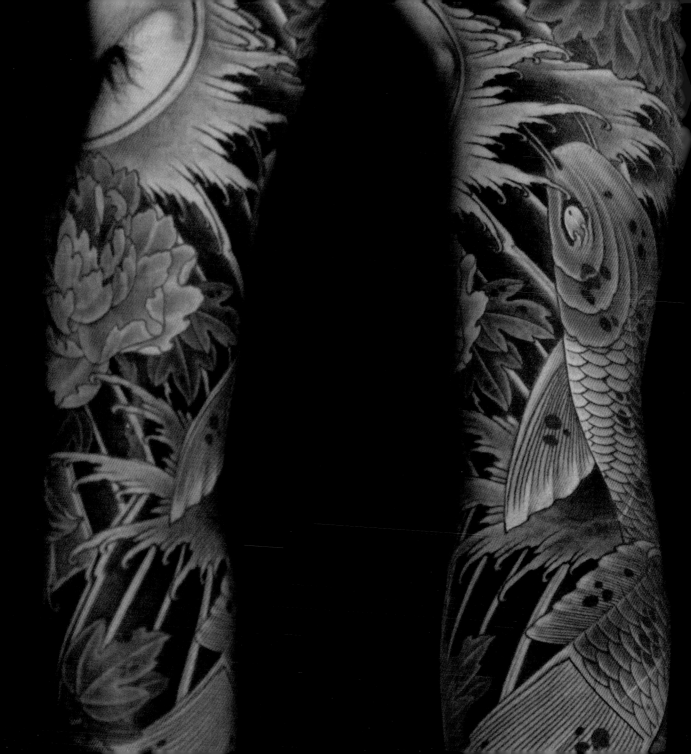

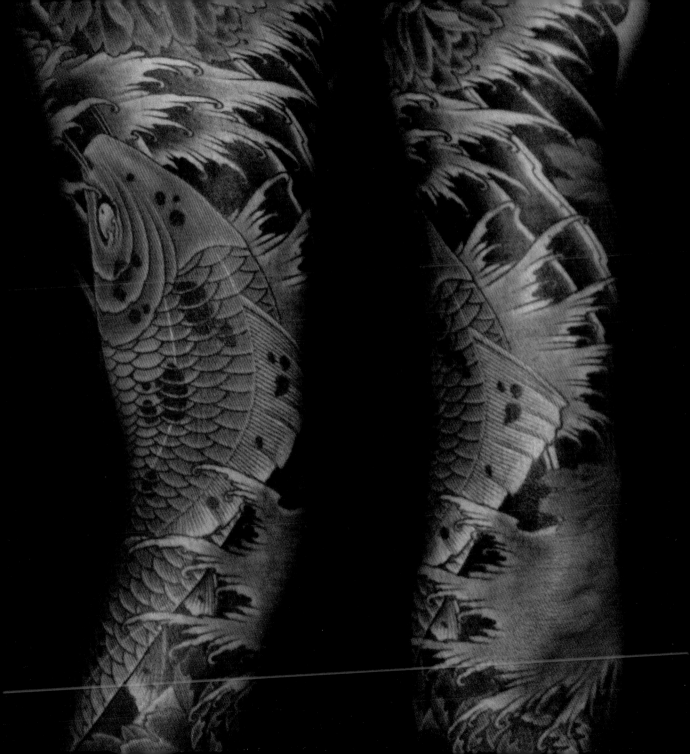

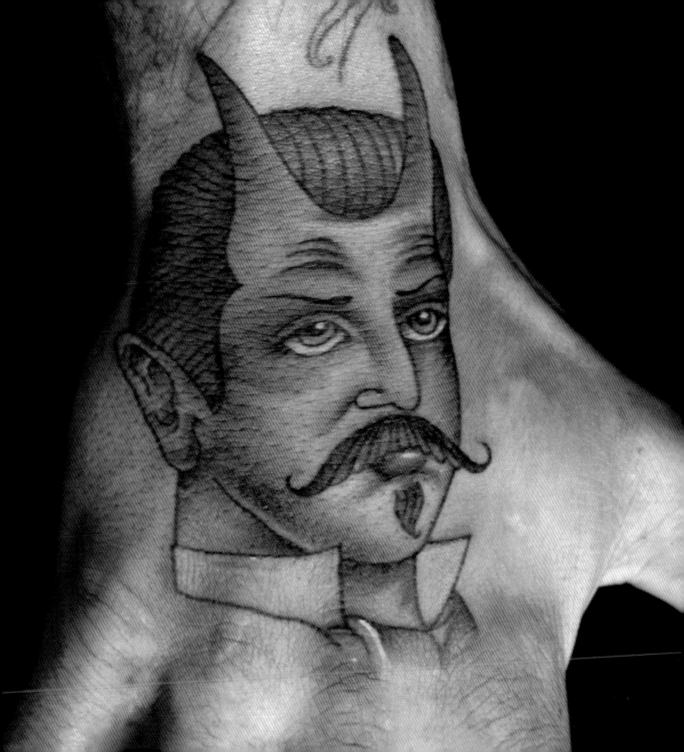

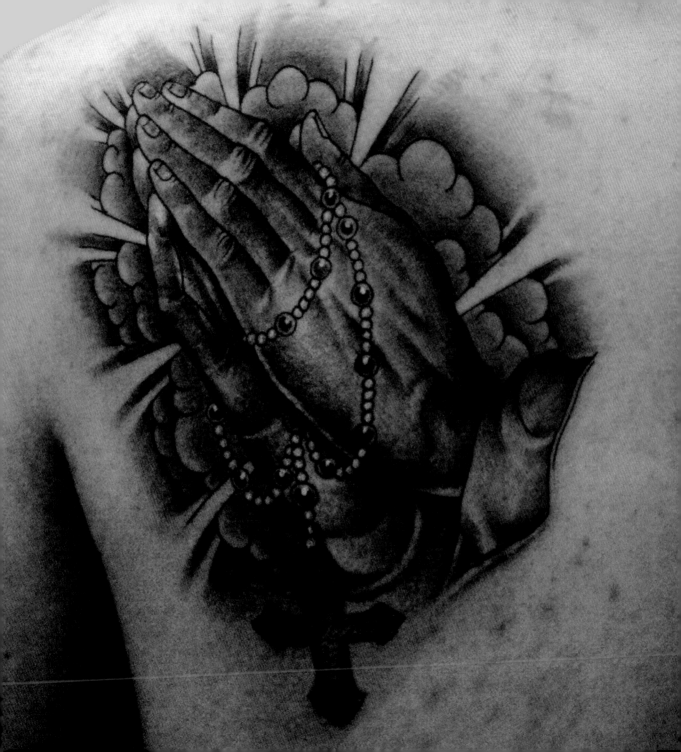

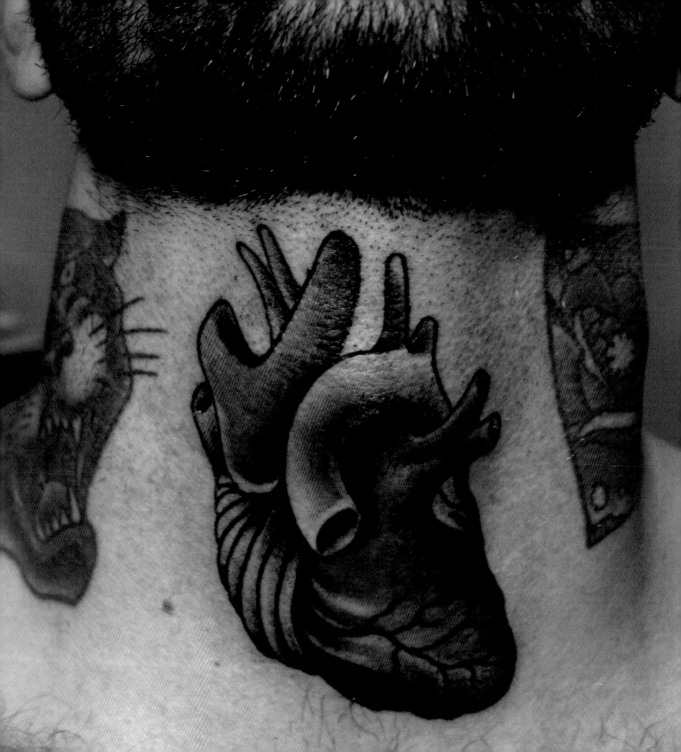

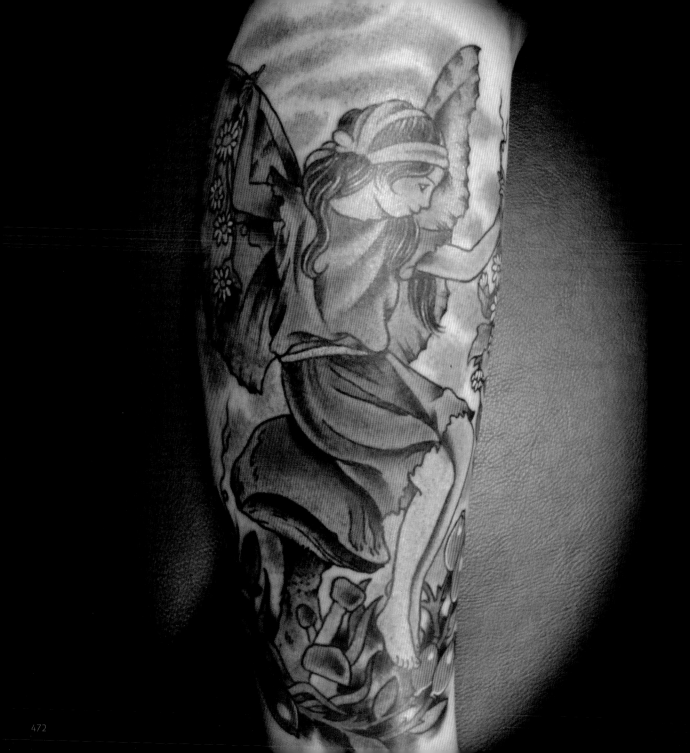

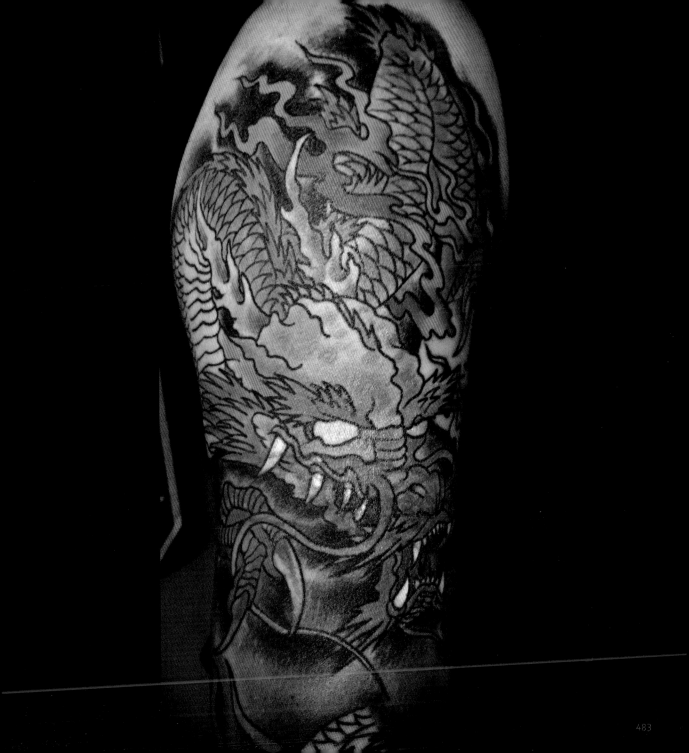

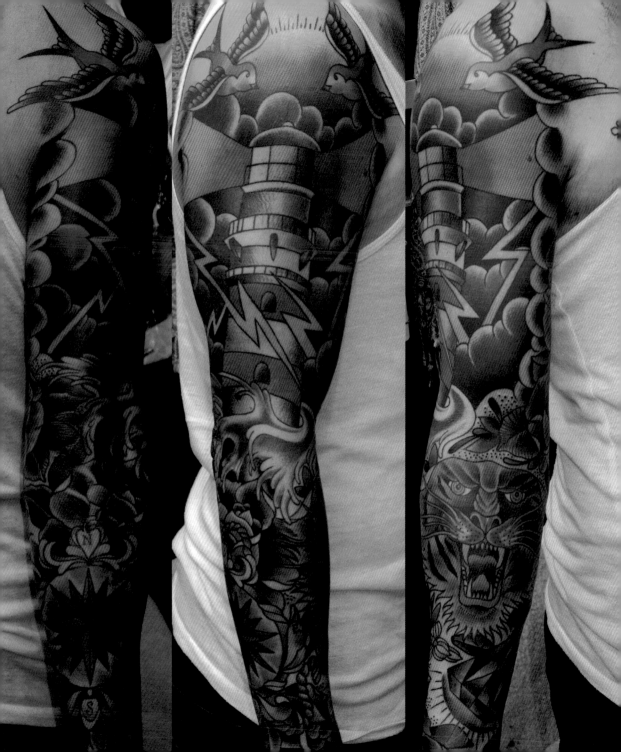

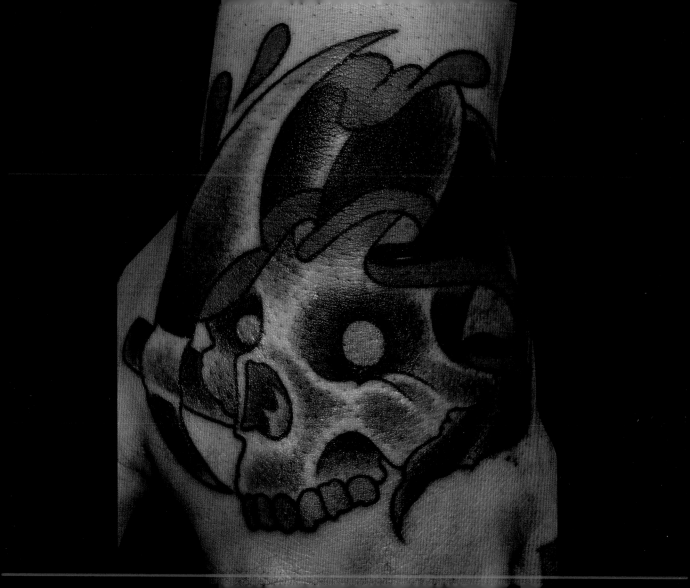

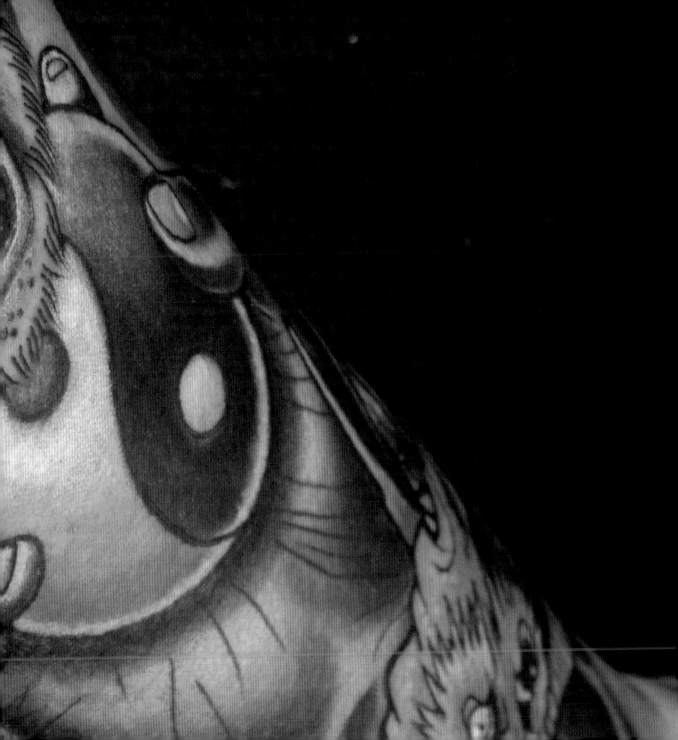

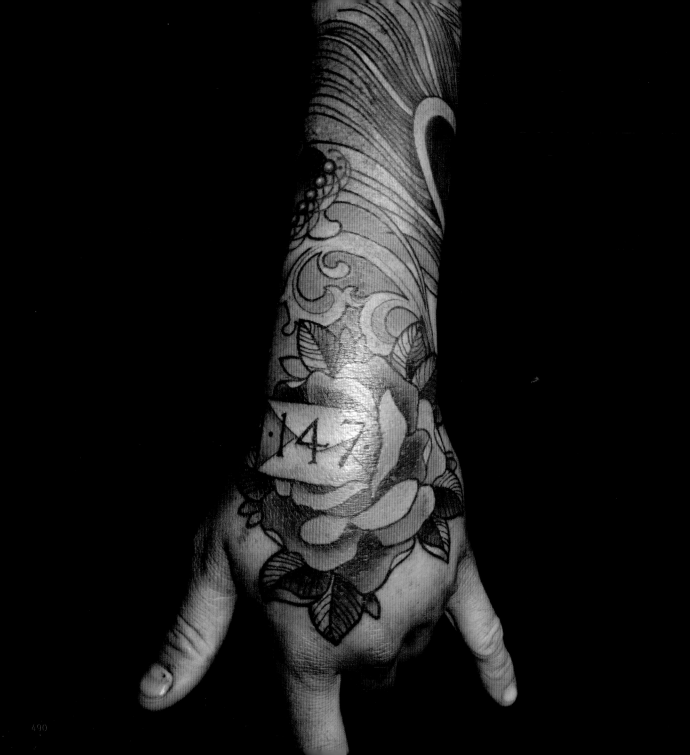

507

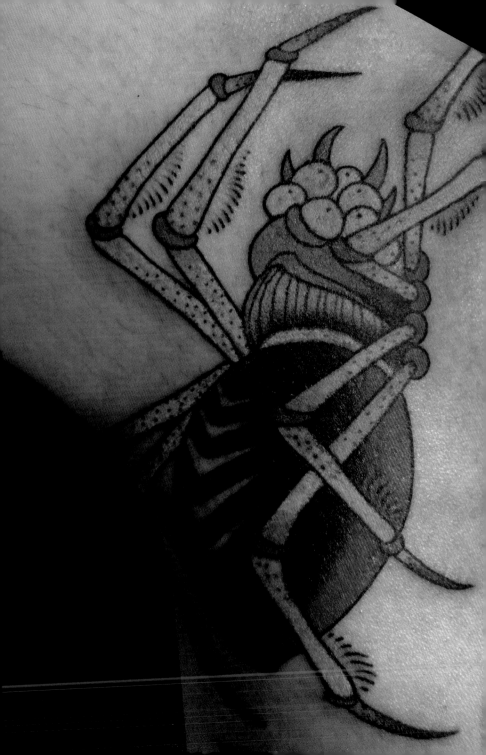

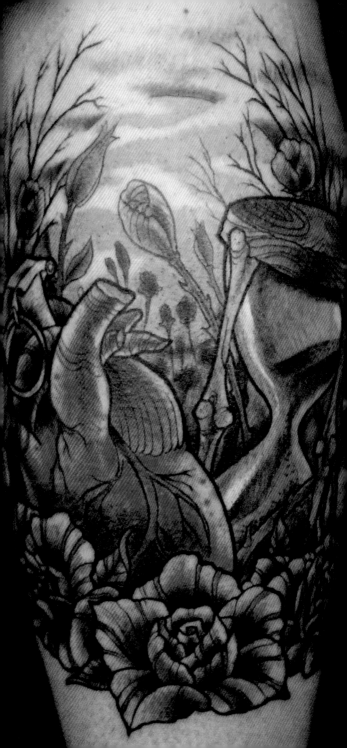

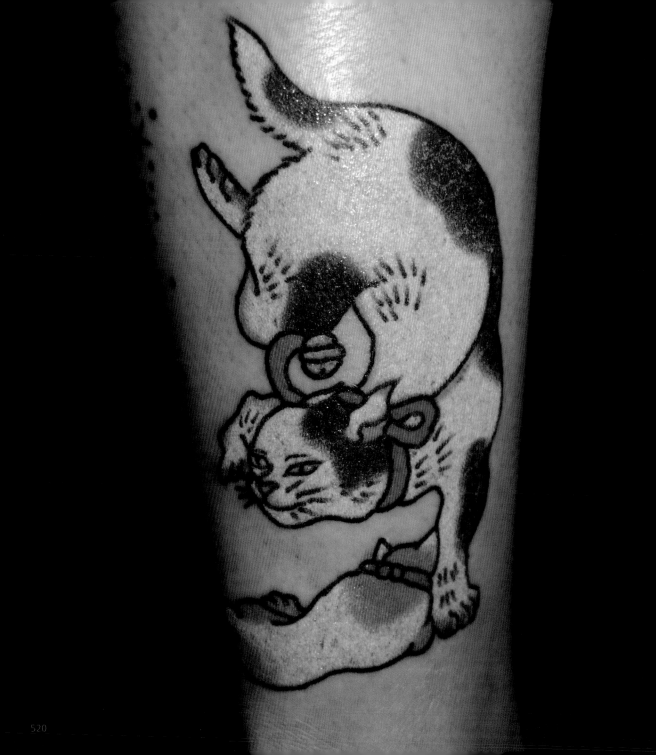

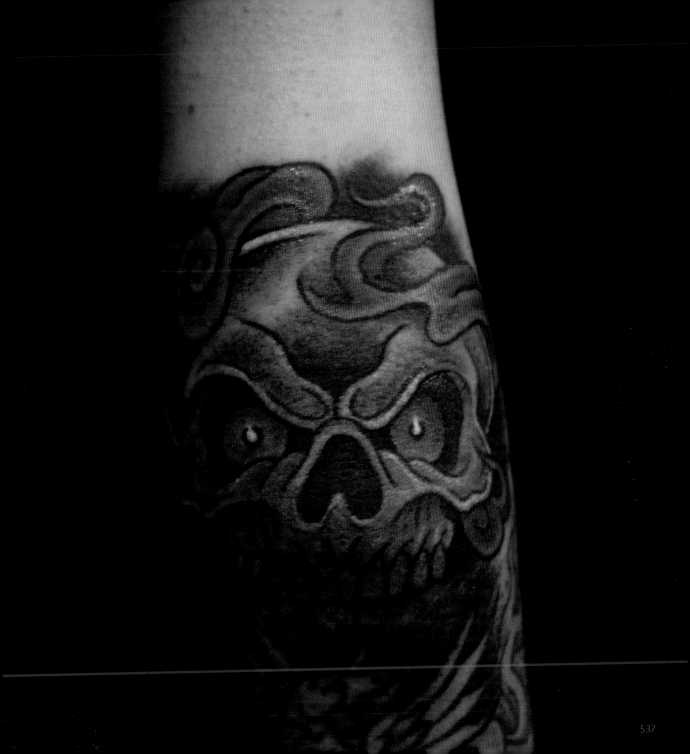

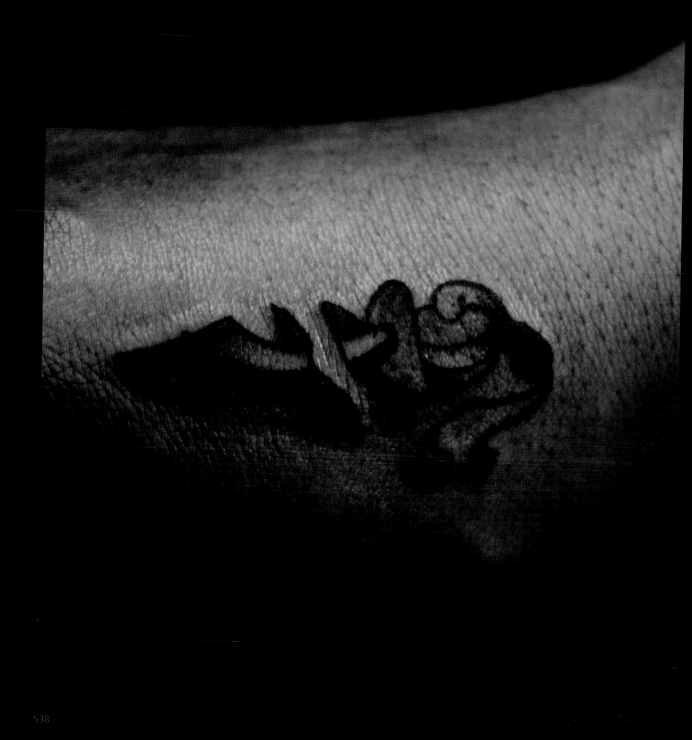

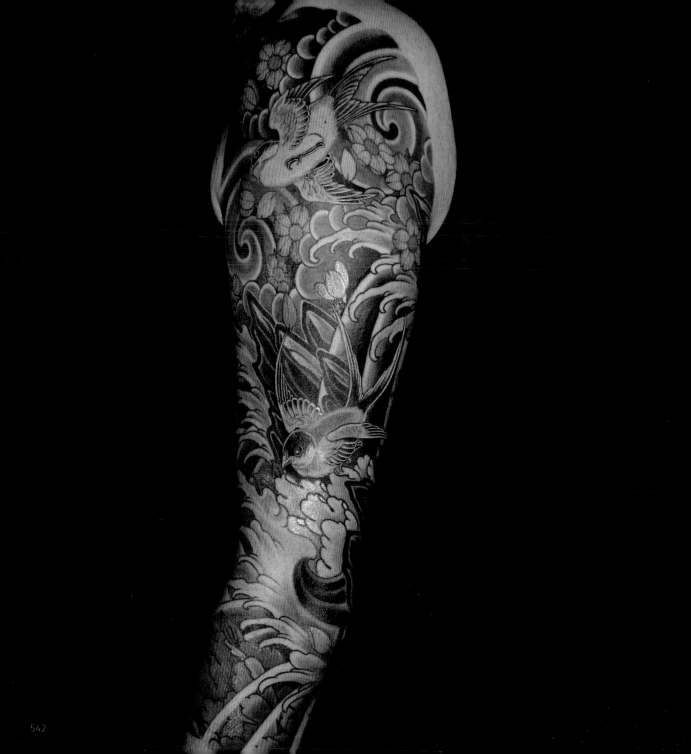

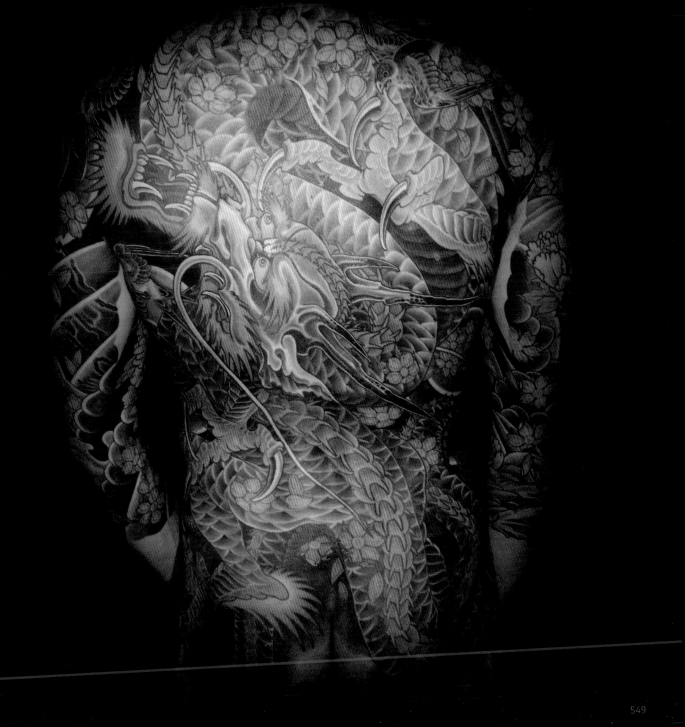

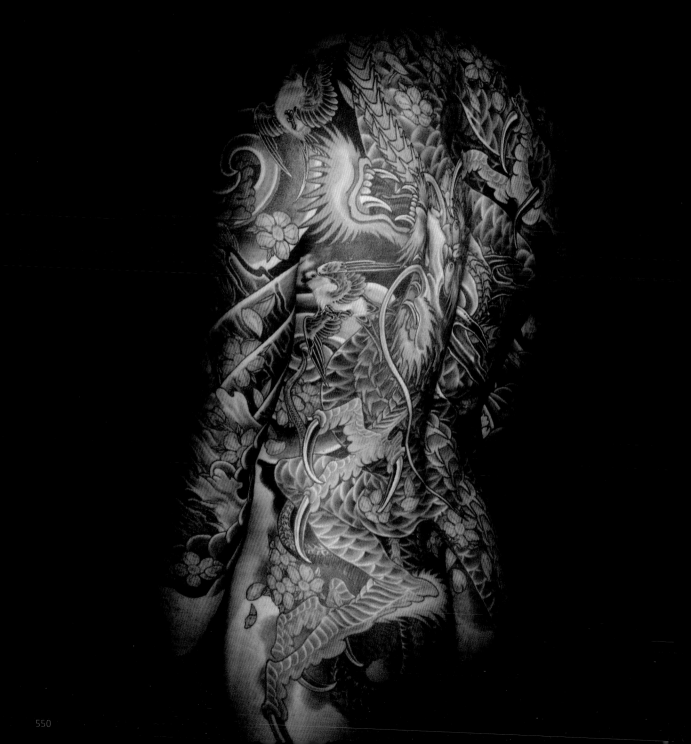

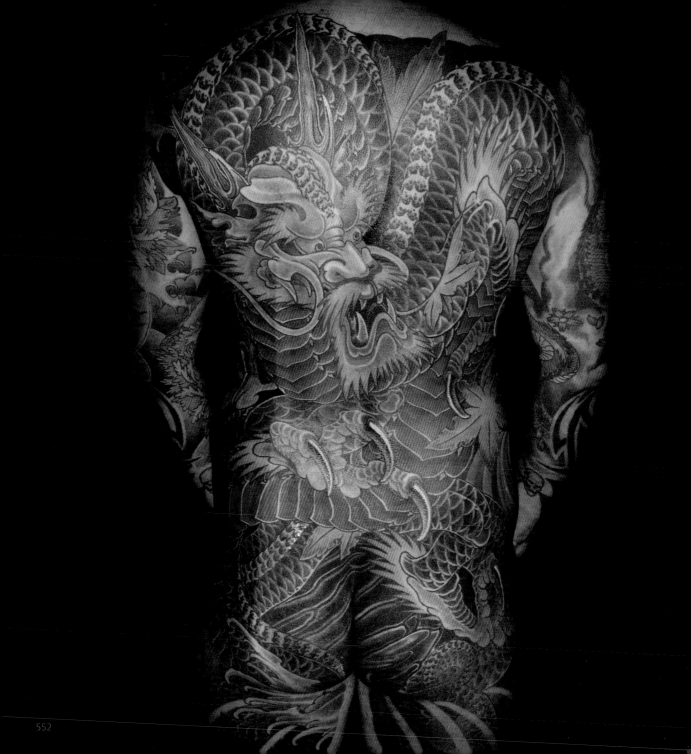

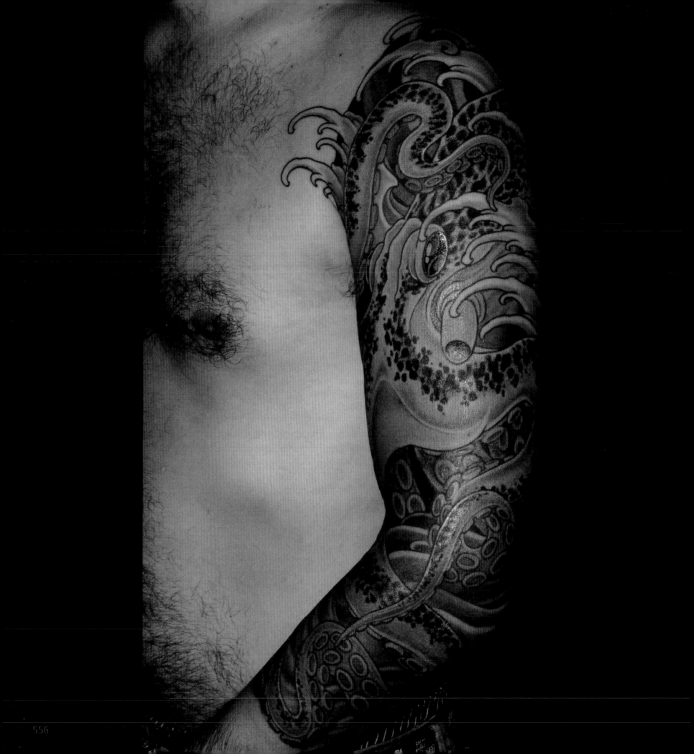

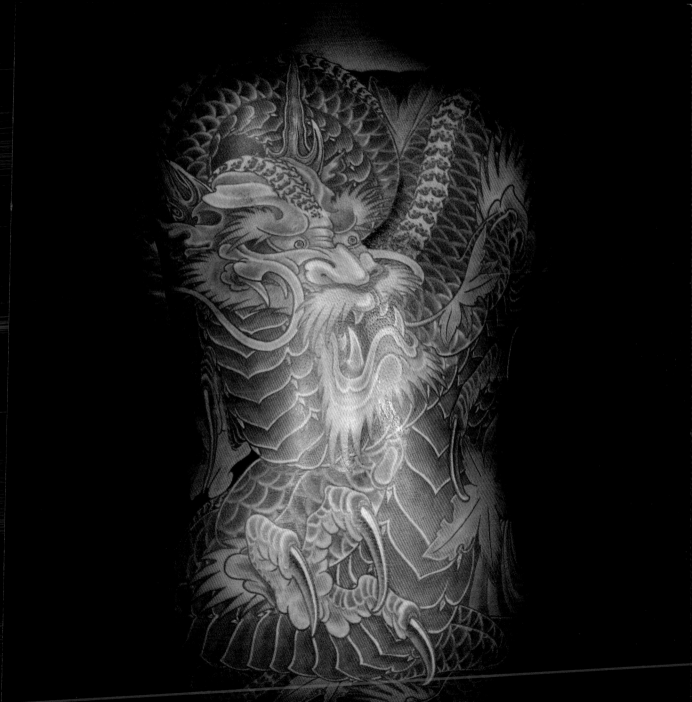

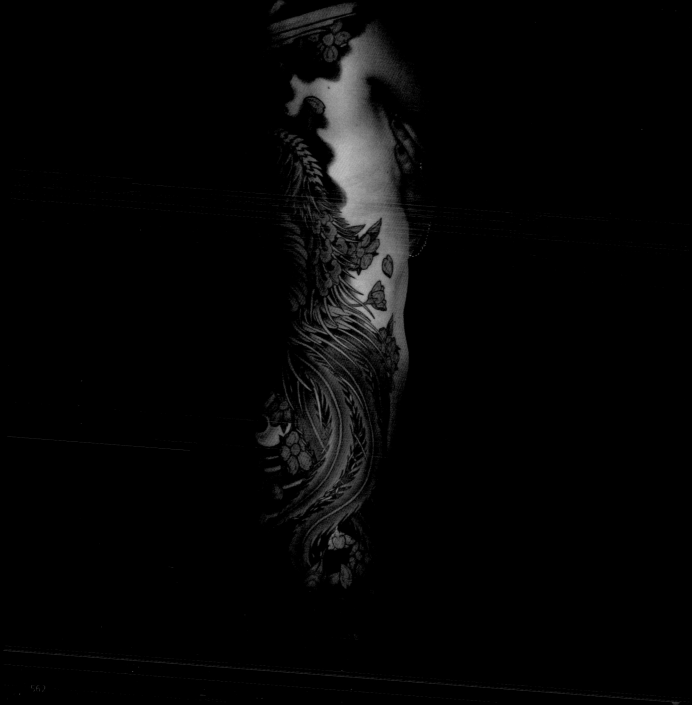

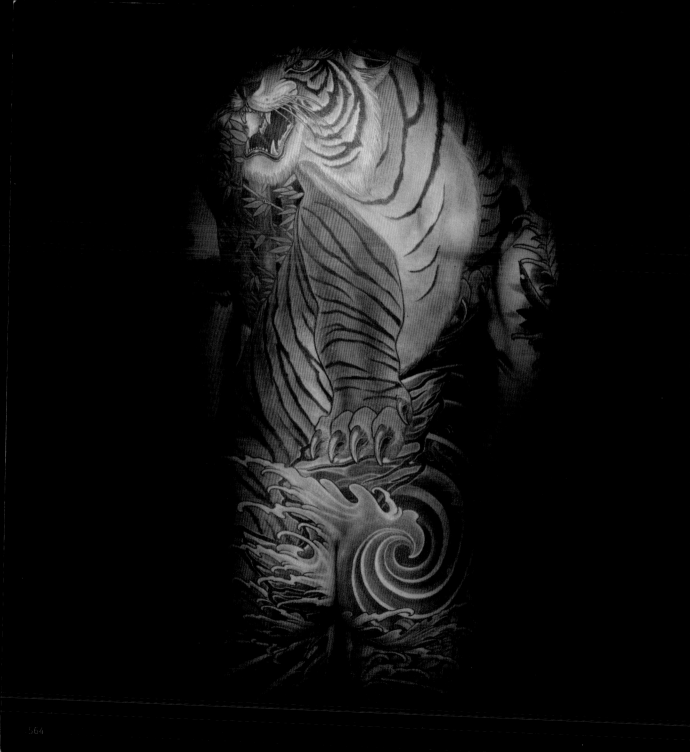

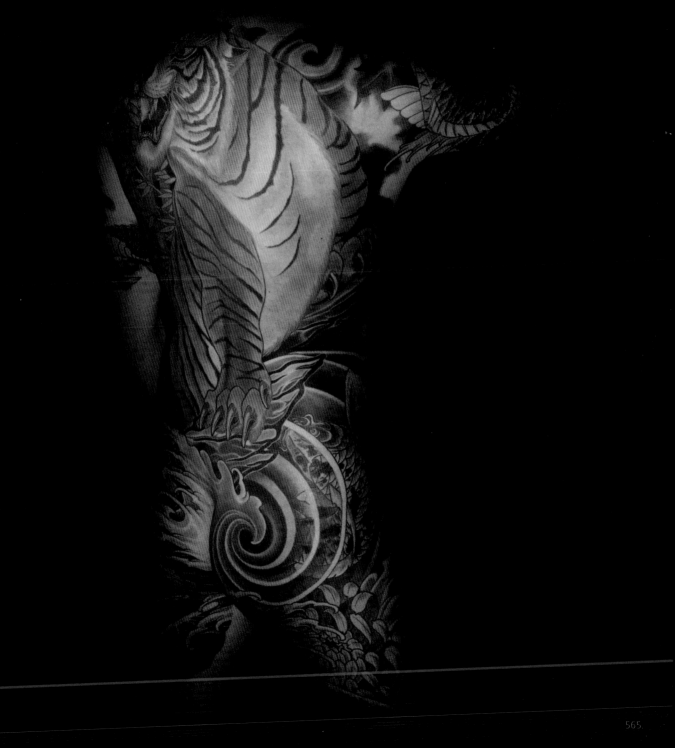

Dorian Serpa
www.facebook.com/dorian.serpa /
www.dorianserpa.blogspot.com
© Dorian Serpa
p 326; 327; 456; 457

En – Genko Tattoo
www.genko-tattoo.com
© En
p 215; 310; 311; 312; 313; 314; 315; 316; 317; 318; 319; 320;
321; 322

Fabio Pimentel
www.bbcstudio.com.br
© Fabio Pimentel
p 347; 474; 509

Filip Leu – The Leu Family's Family Iron
www.leufamilyiron.com
© The Leu Family's Family Iron © 2012
p 18; 19; 20; 21; 22; 23; 184; 185

Garcia Leonam – Ink Karma Nation
www.inkarma.wordpress.com
© Garcia Leonam
p 352; 353; 354; 355; 356; 357; 358; 359

Hata – Inkrat Tattoo
www.inkrattattoo.com
© Hata
p 524; 525; 526; 527; 528; 529; 530; 531; 541

Henning Jørgensen
www.royaltattoo.com
© Henning Jørgensen
p 381; 386; 387

Henrik Grysbjerg – Henrik Tattoo
www.henrik-tattoo.com
© Henrik Grysbjerg
p 15; 360; 361; 362; 363; 364; 365; 366; 367; 368; 369; 370;
371; 372; 373, 374; 375

Jamie Ruth
www.jamieruth.com
© Jamie Ruth
p 334; 335; 336; 337; 338; 339; 340; 341; 342; 343;
344; 345; 346

Jacqueline Spoerlé – Corazon Tattoo
www.corazontattoo.ch
© Jacqueline Spoerlé
p 63; 68; 69; 70; 71; 72; 73; 74; 75; 76; 78; 79; 461

Jondix
www.holytrauma.com
© Jondix
p 80; 81; 82; 83; 84

Jonny – King Carlos Tattoo
www.kingcarlostattoo.com
© Jonny Wemmenstedt
p 332; 333; 484; 485; 486; 487

Kian Forreal – Authent/Ink
www.kianforreal.com
© Kian Forreal
p 188; 382; 383; 384; 385; 420; 421; 422; 423

Kisio - Coru-Family
www.TatauStudio.de/
CoruFamily@web.de
© Coru-Family
p 278; 279; 280; 281; 282; 283; 284; 285

Kostas Tzikalagias – Dirty Roses Tattoo Studio
www.dirtyroses.gr
© Kostas Tzikalagias
p 186; 187; 302; 303; 304; 305; 306; 307; 308; 309

La Astrid
www.1969tattoo.no
© La Astrid
p 230; 231; 232; 233; 234; 235; 236; 237; 238; 239;
240; 241; 242; 243; 244; 245; 246; 247; 248; 330; 331

Robert
www.allstyle-tattoo.de
www.oldschooltattoo-berlin.de
© Robert Broch
p 12

Sailor Bit
www.ethno-tattoo.com
© Sailor Bit
p 542; 543; 544; 545; 546; 547; 548; 549; 550; 551; 552;
553; 554; 555; 556; 557; 558; 559; 560; 561; 562; 563;
564; 565

Sam Clark
www.samclarktattoos.wordpress.com
© Polly Howell
p 488; 490; 491; 494; 495; 496; 497; 498; 499; 500; 501;
502; 503; 504; 505

Sasha Aleksandar – Orca Sun Tattoo
www.orcasuntattoo.com
© Sasha Aleksandar
p 216; 217; 218; 219; 220; 221; 222; 223; 224: 225; 226;
227; 228; 229; 398; 399; 400; 401; 408; 409

Scott Irwin – Scott Irwin Art
www.scottirwinart.com
© Scott Irwin
p 350

Sergey Bardadim – Bardadim Tattoo Art
www.bardadim.com
© Sergey Bardadim / Yana Bardadim
p 388; 389; 418; 419; 434; 435; 458; 459; 460; 462; 514;
515; 516; 517

Shige
www.yellowblaze.net
© Shige
p 8; 30; 31; 32; 33; 34; 35; 36; 37; 38; 39; 40; 41; 42; 43;
44; 45; 46; 47; 48; 49; 50; 51; 52; 53; 54; 55

Tane Legah - Coru-Family
www.TatauStudio.de
CoruFamily@web.de
© Coru-Family
p 286; 287; 288; 289; 290; 291; 292; 293

Tomasi Sulu`ape – Sulu`ape Ink
www.tatau-samoa.com/ www.malofie.org/
www.paulo-suluape-award.com
© Günter Laugisch/ Tomasi Sulu`ape
p 7; 166; 167; 168; 169; 170; 171; 172; 173; 174; 175; 176;
177; 178; 179; 180; 181; 182; 183

Tony – Custom Tattoo by Tony
www.tonystattoos.blogspot.de
© Tony
p 348; 349

alt//cramer
publishing

© 2012 alt//cramer berlin
published by alt//cramer gmbh
Oranienstraße 161
10969 Berlin
p +49 (0)30 616 228 – 222
f +49 (0)30 616 228 – 888
www.altcramer.com mail@altcramer.com

team:
editor: Maria Keilig
layout/imaging/pre-press: Finn Göpfert (elrebel)

if you would like to propose works to include in our upcoming books,
please email us at mail@altcramer.com

created and distributed in cooperation with Frechmann Kolón GmbH
www.frechmann.com

distribuito in Italia da:

© Logos, 2012
Strada Curtatona 5/2
41126 Modena
T. +39 059 412 648
E-mail: commerciale@logos.info
www.libri.it - www.logosedizioni.it

isbn 978-3-942860-08-6
isbn 978-88-576-0454-1 (Logos Italy)
isbn 978-2-8099-0708-7 (Place des Victoires France)

printed in china